What Angels Wish They Knew

Alistair Begg

What Angels Wish They Knew

The Basics Of True Christianity

MOODY PRESS

CHICAGO

All Scripture quotations, unless indicated, are taken from the *Holy Bible: New International Version*®. NIV®. Copyright © 1973, 1978, 1984 by International Bible Society. Used by permission of Zondervan Publishing House. All rights reserved.

The "NIV" and "New International Version" trademarks are registered in the United States Patent and Trademark Office by International Bible Society. Use of either trademark requires permission of International Bible Society.

Scripture quotations marked (PHILLIPS) are reprinted with the permission of Simon & Schuster from *The New Testament in Modern English*, Revised Edition, translated by J. B. Phillips. Copyright © 1958, 1960, 1972 by J. B. Phillips; and by permission of Harper-Collins *Publishers* Limited.

Scripture quotations marked (NKJV) are taken from the New King James Version. Copyright © 1979, 1980, 1982 by Thomas Nelson, Inc. Used by permission. All rights reserved.

Scripture quotations marked (NASB) are taken from the New American Standard Bible © 1960, 1962, 1963, 1968, 1971, 1972, 1973, 1975, 1977, and 1994 by The Lockman Foundation, La Habra, Calif. Used by permission.

Scripture quotations marked (KJV) are taken from the King James Version.

The text of Anna Russell's "Psychiatric Folk Song" is taken from Roy Clements, *The Strength of Weakness* (Fearn, Ross-shire, Scotland: Christian Focus Publications, 1994).

ISBN: 0-8024-1718-3

3 5 7 9 10 8 6 4 2

Printed in the United States of America

With gratitude to God
For every fond memory
of
John George Weir Begg
Harold Glenn Jones

2 Timothy 4:7

Contents

Acknowledgments

Once again I have discovered that, as in the rest of life, so in a writing project, no man is an island. Although I spent periods of time isolated from family and colleagues, I was never outside the realm of their encouragement and prayerful involvement. For all the times my fellow elders asked *how* rather than *where* I was; for the Tuesday morning prayers of the ladies in the office, I am deeply thankful.

I cannot and should not tire of thanking Greg Thornton, Jim Bell and Bill Thrasher for their brotherly affection, their godly wisdom, and their apparently unlimited patience. To Anne Scherich, a special thank-you for her editorial pen, wielded with Christian grace and compassion.

I am equally indebted to the encouragement and example of so many who took me under their wing and taught me how to share my faith, among them Wes Hurd, Doug Olsen, John Shearer and the late Bud Hinkson. In my late teens and early twenties I relished the privilege of listening to the late David Watson and to Michael Green and John Stott, especially when they were preaching evangelistically. I humbly acknowledge my dependence upon so much that they have said and written.

Finally, to Susan, for her prayers and encouragement and for her proofreading and helpful observations, I am on this third occasion more thankful than ever.

1
Mocha, Biscotti, and the Search for Meaning

We live in an age that grants plausibility to every idea and certainty to none. Wander the malls, browse the bookstores, explore the Internet and I think you will find it hard to disagree. The more unusual the idea, the greater the possibility of its being heard and considered. This is one explanation for the sales boom in books that describe matters such as conversations with God, the activities of angels, and even fascinating encounters with fairies and elves. Growing up, as I did, with a story-telling Irish grandfather, I was very familiar with tales of "the little people" living at the bottom of the garden. He also told me sad and chilling stories from the frontline trenches of the First World War.

It was very clear to both of us when he moved from fact to fiction. If there had ever been a moment when I thought my grandfather was serious about these "fairy stories," then I should have had difficulty falling asleep! How quickly times have changed. I recently overheard a lady explain to her friend that her son and daughter-in-law had asked her to read Bible stories to her grandchildren when she was baby-sitting. "Of course," the lady volunteered to her friend, "I don't believe them to be true, but they do make good stories." Tonight youngsters will fall asleep doubting history and trusting mythology.

It was the grandmother in the group who attracted my attention. Actually, not her so much. What caught my eye was the "thing" on her shoulder. My wife and I and our two teenage daughters were nestled into a booth in a crowded local restaurant. From our vantage point we were able to savor the sights and sounds of the lunchtime throng. A young couple negotiating their wriggling firstborn into a high chair. University students huddled over books and eggs. A Chinese mother and her two dark-eyed daughters with shining hair. Skin tone, bone structure, accent, and language all blending as one tiny part of this "great experiment in democracy" sat down to lunch. Directly across from us was a family. Maybe three generations, certainly two, were around the table. A small man with kindly, crinkly eyes was presiding—and probably paying! At the other end of the table and closest to us was a lady, presumably his wife, and it was she who was wearing the "thing" on her shoulder.

"What does that lady have on her shoulder?" I inquired quietly. Quite matter-of-factly Michelle replied, "That's her guardian angel!" "Her what?!" "Oh yes, you can see them all over the place. Men wear them on their lapels, ladies on their scarves or purses." "What do these little metal angels do?" I followed up. "Do people think it's true?" As our conversation wound down, it was apparent that whether it was "true" or not depended largely on the belief of the individual. For most, if it *seemed* true, that was considered good enough.

In light of this, it is no surprise to find a growing interest in books such as *The Elves of Lily Hill Farm*. The author, Penny Kelly, describes her enduring relationship and regular conversations with a small clan of elves led by Alvey, a twenty-two-inch tall spirit in baggy pants and feathered hat. The extent to which credulity is abandoned and the imagination stretched to the breaking point is also witnessed in Neale Walsch's two books of *Conversations with God*. The fact that there is no way of verifying the writer's claims has not been enough to prevent both books appearing simultaneously on the *New York Times* best-sellers list. When questioned about the believability of these "conversations," Walsch declares, "I don't really care what you believe. I am not trying to convince people of anything, and so what people believe on some level is irrelevant. I'm simply sharing."[1] Since, according to recent surveys,[2] more than one in three American adults says that God speaks to them directly, Walsch simply records what a number of his readers claim to have experienced.

Los Angeles Times religion writer Russell Chandler reports that "roughly 30 million Americans—about one in four—now believe in reincarnation, and 14 percent endorse the work of spirit mediums."[3] "A 1978 Gallup poll indicated that ten million Americans were engaged in some aspect of Eastern mysticism and nine million in spiritual healing."[4] There is an undeniable interest in spiritual matters.

Whereas thirty years ago it was a challenge to turn casual conversation with a stranger toward spiritual matters, today the subject is regularly just below the surface waiting to be introduced at any moment by either party. In the sixties a conversation about Zen or other forms of Eastern religion was possible with a bell-bottomed, barefoot hippie. Today your next-door neighbor is just as likely to be part of the curious amalgamation of people and concepts that make up what is referred to as the New Age Movement.

The impact of New Age beliefs and values is pervasive. It provides a way for the individual to combine an interest in very contemporary self-help ideas with very ancient spiritism and very fashionable Eastern mysticism. Part of the appeal is the tolerant flexibility of it all. Instead of being forced to choose from a menu of limited options, we are encouraged to assemble our own spiritual sandwich by creating novel combinations. A little Buddhist stress on tolerance, a dash of Hindu reincarnation, a sprinkling of Christian love, and a thin layer of Scientology. Despite the fact that there are serious disagreements between each of these groups on points of foundational importance, they remain largely ignored. Holding mutually contradictory ideas is one of the characteristics of the contemporary mind-set. From this perspective, spirituality is private and almost inevitably self-serving. This allows us the luxury of conceiving of God on our own terms. So we believe "what we like," and what most of us "like" is the idea of a god who exists for us. Far less attractive is the "outmoded" notion of a personal Creator-God who made us and to whom we are accountable. Yet it was this awareness which arrested Augustine as he lived a life of sensual indulgence: "O God, you have made us for yourself, and our hearts are restless until they find their rest in you."

It is hard to argue with the idea that although Augustine lived long ago and far away, restlessness is still a distinguishing feature of our lives individually and collectively as a society. Airport terminals are increasingly crowded, and the freeways are full of travelers who are searching for "the place" where things are less mundane and more magical. Neil Young speaks for many more than himself when he considers packing it in, buying a pickup, and heading out to L.A. Our lives might be described as bouncing back and forth between superficial optimism and debilitating pessimism. The former is caricatured in the story of the man who fell out of a window on the fortieth floor. As he tumbled earthward, someone on the nineteenth floor heard him shouting, "So far so good!" The latter is cynically conveyed in the story of the New York policeman who came upon a young man standing on the parapet of a bridge over the Hudson River. "What are you doing up there?" inquired the policeman. "I'm going to jump and end my life, it is so pointless and miserable." The policeman talked the young man into rethinking his position. "Let's take twenty minutes," said the policeman. "You take ten to explain why you think life is so empty, and I'll take ten to give you reason for hope." And so they talked for twenty minutes—and then both of them jumped off the bridge!

Most of us manage one way or another to find the point of stable equilibrium between these two extremes. At least for a while. And then, like a wind picking up from nowhere, a sense of restlessness begins to blow us apart. Instead of finding the answers, as Dylan suggested, "blowing in the wind," it proves to be a cold, questioning blast. The same neglected questions are back, crowding us and making us painfully aware of our inability to provide satisfactory answers. Who am I? Does my life have meaning? What happens when I die? Does anyone have the answer to the riddle of life? If there is a God, does He know me and care about me? Is it possible to know Him?

Absent any reasonable explanation of where we came from, why we're here, and where we're going, we are struck, not so much by life's tragedy, but by its apparent triviality. On our darkest days we are left trying to shake the paralyzing thought that at so many levels life can appear to be nothing more than a dirty trick, a fast track to oblivion. The mourning millions at the time of the death of Diana, The Princess of Wales, gave expression, not simply to their affection for her but also to the prevailing sense of hopelessness with which they view the passing of life.

When the singer-songwriter Sting acknowledges that some would say he was a lost man in a lost world, it is on account of the fact that he admits to having lost his faith in science, progress, and religion. In doing so he captures the sense of profound aimlessness that Generation X shares with their parents. The singer's only "salvation" is found in his relationship with his lover. He recognizes that if he were to ever lose his faith in her, then there would be nothing left for him at all. And that is exactly where so many people are living their lives today. Friday's newspaper has a whole section devoted to helping thousands as they search for a meaningful relationship. Unfulfilled and restless, they resolve, with F. Scott Fitzgerald's Gatsby, that "tomorrow we will run faster and stretch out our arms farther." But to what end, if they are unsure of their destination, and if what they reach for continues to elude them? So many of the streets down which we have run in search of meaning are dead ends. Or, to borrow a metaphor from an earlier era in camping, the tent pegs we used to hold the guide ropes of our lives have been uprooted, and we find ourselves blown along, grabbing for anything that might arrest our drift.

One of those tent pegs was *reason*. Toward the end of the Enlightenment, Kant suggested that a fitting motto for that era was "Dare to Know." The problem, plainly put, was this: the more we learned, the worse we felt! By the time we reached the middle of the twentieth century, Bertrand Russell and Albert Einstein in delivering their manifesto at the Caxton Hall, London, provided what would have been regarded today as a perfect sound bite when they declared, "We have found that the men who know most are the most gloomy."

Another tent peg was *science*. Here, we were told, was a viable alternative to religion. Here was the key to both guide and understand our future. But in all honesty, as wonderful and exciting as the discoveries of science have been, they have not provided satisfying answers to the most basic questions. Personal friends who have spent a lifetime in medical science are most keen to talk about spiritual and supernatural ideas because they humbly admit to having raised more questions than answers. They would concur with the warning from Ralph Lapp: "No one—not even the most brilliant scientist alive today—really knows where science is taking us. We are aboard a train which is gathering speed, racing down a track on which there are an unknown number of switches leading to unknown destinations. No single scientist is in the engine cab and there may be demons at the switch. Most of society is in the caboose looking backward."[5]

Another tent peg was a belief in *progress,* the idea that just around the next bend we were going to get things right. Man and nature were moving together to higher and higher levels of life. Darwin's evolutionary hypothesis was in sync with the Beatles, when they told us it's getting better, getting a little better all the time. There is no question that the last hundred years have seen staggering progress and discovery in science and technology. But we must also factor in Auschwitz and apartheid, social disintegration and moral failure. When, as today, the newspaper headline reads, "Fourteen-Year-Old Accused of Killing His Son," it is hard to embrace the belief in progress.

A fourth tent peg was the belief in the *self.* The suggestion that man is self-sufficient is eroded at every point on the journey of life. "Man finds himself dwarfed bodily by the vast stretches of space and belittled temporally by the long reaches of time."[6] As Isaiah the prophet declared, "All men are like grass, and all their glory is like the flowers of the field; the grass withers and the flowers fall." Samuel Beckett captures man's lack of significance in the play *Breath.* Thirty seconds in duration, with no actors, dialogue, or props on the stage. All that's in view is a collection of garbage, and the whole script is the sigh of human life from a baby's cry to a man's last gasp before the grave.

Is there then no possibility of a permanent point of stable equilibrium between the extremes of superficial optimism and debilitating pessimism? Are we condemned to live unable to explain ourselves or our universe? Shall we just embrace the skepticism of Chios, a fourth-century Greek philosopher, when he affirmed that there were only two things that man could know: "None of us knows anything, not even when we know or do not know, nor do we know whether knowing and not knowing exist, nor in general whether there is anything or not."[7] You're not likely to see that quote on an inspirational poster anytime soon! In fact just about now we may find ourselves exclaiming, "Beam me up, Scotty. There are no signs of intelligent life down here!"

The sustained fascination with *Star Trek* may be more significant than we think, especially when we consider the enormous following that exists for science fiction. Popularized by films like *ET, Close Encounters of the Third Kind,* and the *Star Wars* series, an interest in UFOs and the paranormal flourishes as millions keep a weekly appointment with *The X Files*. While, for many, this may be nothing more than a flight of fancy, for others it is expressive of a genuine search for something or someone from "out there" who may be able to rescue us from the mess we find ourselves in "down here." Michael Green quotes Fellini, the celebrated Italian film director, with reference to this:

> Like many people, I have no religion. I am just sitting on a small boat, drifting with the tide. I just go on cutting, editing, shooting, looking at life, trying to make others see that today we stand naked and more

defenseless than at any time in history. What I am waiting for I do not know—perhaps the Martians will come to save us.[8]

This longing for a rescuer from outside is part of the explanation for the fascination with angels during the nineties. Nancy Gibbs, writing in *Time* magazine, describes the extent to which angels have lodged in the popular imagination. "There are angels-only boutiques, angel newsletters, angel seminars. . . . Harvard Divinity School has a course on angels; Boston College has two. Bookstores have had to establish angel sections. In *Publisher's Weekly*'s religious best-seller list, five of the 10 paperback books are about angels."[9] According to a *Time* poll, 69 percent of Americans believe in angels. Even Hillary Clinton is reputed to wear a gold angel on her shoulder on days she needs help. Gibbs refers to this fascination as a "grassroots revolution of the spirit in which all sorts of people are finding all sorts of reasons to seek answers about angels for the first time in their lives."

Instead of these angels appearing as powerful, even fearful creatures, the New Age versions are mellow and definitely nonthreatening. Apparently no one has encountered any of the fearless soldiers-with-flashing-swords variety to which we are introduced in the Bible. In direct contrast, says Gibbs, "For those who choke too easily on God and his rules, theologians observe, angels are the handy compromise, all fluff and meringue, kind, nonjudgmental. And they are available to everyone, like aspirin."

Already it seems that the fascination with angels is on the wane. This is in part because so many of the claimed encounters appear to owe a little too much to a fertile imagination. In saying this, we must admit that for the skeptic no proof is possible, and for the "believer" no proof is necessary. Another reason for the declining interest is simply that it has become fairly obvious that angels are unable to meet our expectations. When we turn to the Bible we discover that this is by design. They are created beings, and they are limited in their powers. They are described as "ministering spirits sent to serve those who will inherit salvation" (Hebrews 1:14). We find one making a night visit to some shepherds, telling them not to be afraid and announcing "good news of great joy" in the coming of a Savior. Another is perched almost cheekily, certainly triumphantly, on the stone which he has rolled away from the tomb of Jesus, not to allow Him to leave but to let others see He was gone! The seasoned soldiers of Rome were frozen in fear before this one whose appearance "was like lightning" and whose clothes were as "white as snow." Two angels were on hand in Jerusalem to inform the men of Galilee who were gazing intently into the sky that Jesus had been taken up into heaven and that they could expect Him to return in the same way they had seen Him go. We are told to expect angels at "the end of the age" to come and weed out of God's kingdom everything that causes sin and all who do evil. In each case the angels are either attending divine events, declaring good news, singing heaven's melodies, defending God's children, or fulfilling divine purposes. This is something far grander than the popular notions of angels cruising the freeways as representatives of some celestial AAA on the lookout for flat tires.

But this is not a book about angels. My purpose is not to address what they are able or unable to do but instead to recognize that there is something angels wish they knew. That something, as we shall see, takes us to the core of biblical theology, which brings us also to the pivotal event of human history. The title of the book is essentially a paraphrase of a sentence from a letter written by Peter, the disciple of Jesus Christ. In writing about salvation he observes, "Even angels long to look into these things" (1 Peter 1:12).

For some of you, this will be a journey down well-trodden paths. I hope there will be fresh insights as you relearn old lessons. Others will come to this material having given Christianity only a passing glance. I hope that this will hold your gaze. Other readers will be unofficial members of what I like to refer to as "agnostics anonymous." Perhaps this will help to answer some of your honest, searching questions. Doubtless there will be others who are living on the borders of cynicism on account of previous encounters with exponents of Christianity. You have all but dismissed it totally because all that you have seen to this point is sandals or scandals: a Christianity that was buried in a first-century world of togas and sandals with no connection whatsoever to your life and times, or a Christianity that was billed as a springboard to health and wealth but whose leaders were captive to their own sexual and financial lusts. I hope that this straightforward statement of the basics will help you to sort out the true from the false.

Whatever point you are starting from, it is important for you to know that what follows is largely descriptive rather than defensive. I have not

attempted to write a defense of the faith. The foot-
notes will point you to those who have done so
superbly. This book will serve best not by answering
every question but by sending us to the one Book
which has the answers. If for some readers my book
provides the final stage in a journey to personal
faith, it will be on account of the groundwork
already laid at prior stages. I don't ever imagine
delivering the following chapters in a classroom.
This is, instead, coffee-shop material. In defining
the context I am not seeking to diminish the content; quite the reverse. Some of the liveliest debate
and the most penetrating insight into life, culture,
and religion is happening all across the country in
the context of coffee and books. These coffee shops
with books, or bookshops with coffee, represent the
missing corners of our cities. Deirdrie Donahue,
writing in *USA Today*, suggests,

> Here's a provocative theory to explain why people
> hang out in bookstores. They have become cultural
> magnets for a fragmented society that no longer gath-
> ers on the front porch or at the corner store. Book-
> stores have become one of the last places where
> people feel safe and mentally enriched . . . and unlike
> clothing stores and record shops, books never make
> you feel fat or old.[10]

Howard Schultz of Starbucks seems to concur
with that idea when he talks about the romantic
notion of creating a new and better world far from
the drabness of everyday life. "That is Starbuck's aim,
too. We try to create in our stores, an oasis, a little
neighborhood spot where you can take a break, listen to some jazz, and ponder universal or personal
or even whimsical questions over a cup of coffee."[11]

This, then, is the context in which I suggest the following chapters are coffee-shop material. These places tend to attract a cross section of our culture that is prepared to listen to all kinds of strange ideas. Here you can rub shoulders with very Western-looking individuals who are dressed in the robes appropriate for Tibetan monks. You can listen in on conversations about spiritism, Scientology, and the healing power of crystals; and you can hear the elaborate claims of alternative medicine being offered alongside the views of faith healers. Every idea is regarded as having plausibility provided no one idea is granted certainty. It is in this environment of mocha, biscotti, and the search for meaning that we urge consideration of what angels wish they knew.

Meanwhile, Back in Athens

Athens would have offered a prime location for a Starbucks. Certainly as a location in which all kinds of ideas about life and death, origins and destinations were announced and considered. For more than five hundred years it had been the number one city in Greece. It had magnificent architecture. Its buildings and monuments were unrivaled. Even today its ruins retain a unique grandeur. It was cluttered with shrines and temples, statues and altars. Greek sculptors had fashioned striking images of the gods, some in gold or silver, others in ivory or marble, and the lesser lights in brass or stone. But they were all beautiful and would have been spellbinding to the average tourist.

The gleaming spearpoint of Athena could be seen glinting in the precincts of the Parthenon from as far away as forty miles. In much the same way that people today take tours of Beverly Hills to have the homes of the "stars" pointed out to them, guides in

Athens could ensure that you would see Apollo, Zeus, Aphrodite, Hermes, Dionysus, Poseidon, Artemis, and Asclepius. The city boasted more gods than all the rest of the country, and the joke was that "in Athens it was easier to find a god than a man." Here, in the intellectual metropolis of the empire there was "a blend of superstitious idolatry and enlightened philosophy."[1]

The Athenians and the foreigners who lived there are described as spending their time doing nothing but talking about and listening to the latest ideas. If we could have listened in on their conversations, we would have found them wrestling with the same issues we face. What is this world? Where did it come from? Where is it going? Why?

In the "minutes book" of the early church (Acts), Luke records the reaction of Paul to what he found in Athens.

> He was greatly distressed to see that the city was full of idols. So he reasoned in the synagogue with the Jews and the God-fearing Greeks, as well as in the marketplace day by day with those who happened to be there. A group of Epicurean and Stoic philosophers began to dispute with him. Some of them asked, "What is this babbler trying to say?" Others remarked, "He seems to be advocating foreign gods." They said this because Paul was preaching the good news about Jesus and the resurrection. Then they took him and brought him to a meeting of the Areopagus, where they said to him, "May we know what this new teaching is that you are presenting? You are bringing some strange ideas to our ears, and we want to know what they mean." (Acts 17:16–20)

Not only were they asking the kinds of questions that are still on the lips of people today, the answers they received are still being offered as we look into century twenty-one. Although Epicurus died in 270 B.C., and his rival, Zeno, seven years later, the ideas of these men remain influential. Epicureanism and Stoicism are around; they are simply in disguise. Allow me to describe them, and I think you will get the picture. The Epicureans believed that the gods had no interest in, and no influence on, human affairs. They regarded the world and everything that happens as due to chance. Death had no encore, and so they encouraged the pursuit of pleasure. "Eat, drink, and be merry, for tomorrow you die!" The sixties slogan "Turn on, tune in, drop out" provides a simplified summary of their view of life. This is the philosophical substance of banal movies like *Wayne's World*, with its call to "Party on, Dude!" Quite apart from the fact that this idea has no solution for death, it is also incapable of satisfaction in life. Those who have surrounded themselves with the most toys are not apparently winning after all.

Suze Orman, author of *The 9 Steps to Financial Freedom*, is honest enough to admit that when she first made enough money to drive a luxury car, wear a Rolex with her designer clothes, and vacation on a private island, it did not bring satisfaction. She felt alone even when she was around good friends. "I had more affluence than I'd ever dreamed of. Yet I felt sad and empty—and at a loss. For if money didn't equal happiness, I had no idea what did."[2]

When, as individuals, we have no satisfying answer for the questions "Where did I come from?" and "Where am I going?" we should not be surprised by our inability to make sense of "the middle." Michael Green quotes the British journalist Bernard Levin, who recognized his dilemma.

> To put it bluntly, have I time to discover why I was born before I die? . . . I have not managed to answer that question yet, and however many years I have before me they are certainly not as many as there are behind. There is an obvious danger in leaving it too late. . . . Why do I have to know why I was born? Because, of course, I am unable to believe that it was an accident, and if it wasn't one, it must have a meaning.[3]

When Robin Williams, as the zealous and unorthodox English teacher in *Dead Poets Society*, constantly urges his students with the cry of "Carpe diem!" (seize the day), it is because he is convinced that death will end it all. If he were simply encouraging the boys to do their best, no one could fault him. The flaw is in the framework. Or perhaps we should say, in the absence of a framework. Life is without design because for the Epicurean there is no designer. Sartre pursues this notion to its logical and tragic end in his first novel, aptly titled *Nausea*. One of its characters, Roquentin, is described walking in the park and being overcome by the nausea of the meaninglessness of life. As he looks around, he concludes, "Every existent is born without reason, prolongs itself out of weakness and dies by chance."

Men and women move around our towns and cities unfulfilled, depersonalized, and ultimately dehumanized. On a bad day you feel like a tiny cog that has fallen and is being rubbed raw by a giant machine over which you have no control. On a better day you derive some slim encouragement from seeing yourself, courtesy of Pink Floyd, as "just another brick in the wall." When we see "No Future" painted on a leather jacket or tattooed on a young man's arm, we are witnessing the fact that for many the only verifiable truth they are willing to affirm is the meaningless absurdity of life.

Epicurus urged his followers to pursue a kind of pleasure that was detached from pain and fear. What he failed to tell them was that the pursuit of pleasure for itself will never bring satisfaction. Such an illegitimate longing is insatiable. It is like drinking sea water. The more you drink, the thirstier you become.

Although only a few people today may have heard of Epicurus, countless numbers live their lives with a similar stress on chance or luck. Consider the lines of people waiting for the chance to purchase what they hope will be the winning ticket in the lottery. Perhaps, they reason, this week they will get the dramatic reversal of fortune which they feel is necessary to make sense of their existence. In the pursuit of such random pleasure in a world where death ends everything, men and women find themselves with nothing to fear and nothing to hope for.

For those who did not like the idea of viewing life as a chance collection of atoms in a chance universe, stoicism offered an alternative. The founder, Zeno, and his followers believed that "the happenings in the world are determined by fate, and a cold, impersonal and merciless thing it is."[4] The Stoics derived their name from the stoa, which was the painted colonnade next to the agora where they taught. These "philosophers of the porch" encouraged self-sufficiency while acknowledging the existence of a supreme being. They referred to this "world soul" in much the same way that people talk about nature today—a blind, impersonal, and rational force which is regarded as somehow directing the affairs of the world.

> Imagining himself to be too sophisticated intellectually to believe in God, modern man speaks of "time and chance" and "Mother Nature" (notice the capital letters). God is naturalized, nature is deified. We rid ourselves of God, but in the process substitute another, poorer deity in his place, becoming indeed like the children of a lesser god. We become just like our long-dead forefathers whose gods were also found in nature.[5]

From this perspective, the very best one might hope for is to resign oneself to the circumstances in the card game of life to play the hand you're dealt.

What is striking about this is the fact that two thousand years later, men and women are still bouncing between these two alternatives. The late F. F. Bruce comments: "Stoicism and Epicureanism represent alternative attempts in pre-Christian paganism to come to terms with life, especially in times of uncertainty and hardship, and post-Christian paganism has not been able to devise anything appreciably better."[6]

It's the roller-coaster ride approach, with its emphasis on chance, escape, and the enjoyment of pleasure versus the Russian roulette alternative, marked by fatalism, self-resignation, and the endurance of pain. In the first instance, the world is viewed as a fluke and its inhabitants are adrift on the sea of chance. In the second case, the world is regarded as being under the control of some impersonal force. Either way, men and women are left facing the inevitable conclusion that they come from plankton soup, subsist for a few years as gene carriers, and then dwindle to nothing like candles when the party is over. Generation X has worked it out. If human beings emerged by chance from a slimy sludge, if they are nothing more than turbocharged apes, if the drama of life is without significance, then they must do what they can, or what they want, to ease the pain of such an existence.

The crowd in Athens were hedging their bets with an idol to an "unknown God." Paul seized the opportunity to offer them an alternative to the frivolity of chance or the malevolence of fate. He told them about a personal Creator-God who is distinct from His creation and yet intimately involved with what He has made. This is how he put it:

> The God who made the world and everything in it is the Lord of heaven and earth and does not live in temples built by hands. And he is not served by human hands, as if he needed anything, because he himself gives all men life and breath and everything else. From one man he made every nation of men, that they should inhabit the whole earth; and he determined the times set for them and the exact places where they should live. God did this so that men would seek him and perhaps reach out for him and find him, though he is not far from each one of us. "For in him we live and move and have our being." As some of your own poets have said, "We are his offspring."
> Therefore since we are God's offspring, we should not think that the divine being is like gold or silver or stone—an image made by man's design and skill. (Acts 17:24–29)

In this speech Paul is challenging the Athenians to rethink their view of the world. Instead of viewing themselves as little more than pawns in a giant chess game, they should consider the fact that they were uniquely and purposefully created. Rather than thinking of history as trailing off into infinite boredom or drifting to a dreadful anticlimax, they might ponder the fact that it is heading for a grand finale when the purpose for which God made the universe has been satisfied. They should consider the fact that the creation is separate from God. It is not coequal with Him, nor is He to be confused with it. Although Paul makes no direct reference to the opening chapters of Genesis, he is underscoring what we find there, not least of all that human beings have been made in the image of God. "So God created man in his own image, in the image of God he created him; male and female he created them" (Genesis 1:27).

Have you ever wondered why we find ourselves in constant search of meaning? Why it is that despite knowing so much about so many things we are not sure that we know ourselves? We are hard-pressed not only to provide a reasonable explanation for our beginnings but also to grant significance to our journey. Such a sense of being forlorn is not the unique prerogative of the addict or the homeless. No, this dark, disturbing doubt is lurking in the ladies' tennis league, it is filed in the briefcase of the entrepreneur, and it flirts with the mind of the serious student.

Why is it that the businessman, after closing a successful deal, can't shake the feeling that there must be something more? Or the golf professional who has worked consistently to secure a position at a prestigious club remains unsatisfied and restless? Why do we find ourselves living with the nagging uncertainty that we have forgotten something? Because we have! Actually, we have forgotten *Someone*.

We should not be surprised that when a society denies the reality of the God of creation it is filled with individuals who do not know who they are and cannot ultimately explain why they do what they do. Alister McGrath makes the point with great forcefulness:

> Because we are created by God in his image, we desire him; because we are sinful, we cannot satisfy that desire ourselves—either by substituting something for God, or by trying to coerce him to come to us. And so a real sense of frustration, of dissatisfaction, develops. And that dissatisfaction—but not its theological interpretation—is part of common human experience.[7]

C. S. Lewis refers to a deep and intense feeling of longing within human beings which no earthly object or experience can satisfy. He illustrated this by referring to the quest for beauty.

> The books or the music in which we thought the beauty was located will betray us if we trust to them; it was not in them, it only came through them, and what came through them was longing. These things— the beauty, the memory of our own past—are good images of what we really desire; but if they are mistaken for the thing itself they turn into dumb idols, breaking the hearts of their worshippers. For they are not the thing itself; they are only the scent of a flower we have not found, the echo of a tune we have not heard, news from a country we have not visited.[8]

It is because we have been made in God's image that we are accorded an astonishing dignity. With this comes responsibility to rule over the earth and to care for the rest of creation in a manner that neither exploits nor abuses nor views all species as being of equal value. We are at the same time, on account of creation, confronted with the fact of our accountability. As we will see, this is a basic reason why people are keen to reject the God of creation and replace Him with idols of their own construction. Six centuries before Christ was born, Jeremiah the prophet described the activities of the people of his day.

> The customs of the peoples are worthless; they cut a tree out of the forest, and a craftsman shapes it with his chisel. They adorn it with silver and gold; they fasten it with hammer and nails so it will not totter. Like a scarecrow in a melon patch, their idols cannot speak; they must be carried because they cannot walk. (Jeremiah 10:3–5)

It is an amazing picture of the foolishness of men and women that articles conceived in their imaginations and created by their own hands should become the objects of their worship. But before we look down our noses at these ancient people, we should pause to consider the fact that now some two and a half thousand years later, we find highly intelligent people exchanging the truth for a lie and worshiping created things rather than the Creator. The reason is simple. Choosing a substitute obviates accountability to God. That is the appeal of idolatry. "We can meet idols on our own terms because they are our own creations. They are safe, predictable, and controllable; they are portable and completely under the user's control." People need only face themselves and manage to explain away their wrongdoing by blaming it on their genes or their environment. This, as we are about to discover, will not do.

Before proceeding, we remind ourselves of what we have discovered. First, that our world is not a cosmic accident. It has been created purposefully by God. Second, as human beings we are not the product of chance. We are not an evolutionary cosmic accident. We have been created by God. The Bible tells us that our place in the universe is as a result of the creative purpose of a personal God. There is a continuity between our finite selves and our infinite Creator, who stands behind the universe as its final source of meaning. There is a qualitative distinction between *man* and animals and plants. As clever and intriguing as chimpanzees may be, we do not observe them doing flower arrangements or constructing stealth bombers! Such creativity is part of our having been made in God's image. It is this which gives us personality, morality, dignity, and value. It is undeniable that from the dawn of history man has by his art and accomplishments distinguished himself from the rest of creation. Neither the humanistic worldview of the West nor the pantheistic worldview of the East can provide a cogent explanation of this uniqueness. The evolutionary concept of an impersonal beginning plus time plus chance fails to answer the deepest questions of life. Men and women find themselves living with alienation, loneliness, and an emptiness that verges on madness. Life is divided into the horrible and the miserable. Now a biblical worldview leads to very different conclusions. Here we find an adequate reason for ascribing a unique value to all human life. The words of Psalm 139 leave us in no doubt concerning this.

You created my inmost being;
>you knit me together in my mother's womb.
I praise you because I am fearfully and wonderfully
>>made;
>your works are wonderful,
>I know that full well.
My frame was not hidden from you
>when I was made in the secret place. . . .
>your eyes saw my unformed body.
All the days ordained for me
>were written in your book
>before one of them came to be.
How precious to me are your thoughts, O God!
>How vast is the sum of them!
Were I to count them,
>they would outnumber the grains of sand.
When I awake,
>I am still with you.

>>>>>(Psalm 139:13–18)

Because we have been created in the image of God we are distinct from all other forms of life. God has written eternity into our minds so that we know that there is something beyond this world. We recognize that history is not cyclical but linear. In other words, we are not just going round and round, lost helplessly in space. Having been made in the image of God, we can affirm the fact of human dignity, but at the same time we are painfully aware that all is not well. This strange duality reveals itself when in one moment we appear angelic and the next beastly; when we find man is capable of building both hospitals and torture chambers. . . . Explanation to follow.

3

Glorious Ruins

𝓈

One of the charming aspects of touring in Scotland is the discovery, often in remote regions, of
ancient castles. While some of them are occupied,
many of them are now ruins. But they continue to
attract our attention and cause us to pause in wonder because, although they have fallen into disre-
pair, there is still a grandeur to them. Ruins they
may be, but they are still possessed of enough of
their former dignity to be justifiably regarded as
"glorious ruins." So it is with man. As offensive as it
may seem to be, the Bible says that we are ruins! On
account of sin, God's image in us has been obscured
but not obliterated. We are still distinguishable
from the rest of creation, and even in our "fallen-
ness" are aware of gifts and are capable of achievements. When John Calvin addressed this, he was
very careful, as we must be, to point out that these
"relics" of the image of God in fallen man afford no
basis for acceptance with God.

"Oh, you don't believe in all that stuff about original sin, do you?" "Well, do you have a better explanation for the way things are?" This is a familiar snippet of dialogue whenever an attempt is made to explain just why there is so much conflict, confusion, exploitation, and abuse in our world. Why do we lie and cheat and boast and steal? How did that precious bundle we brought home from the hospital manage so quickly to muster up such a spirit of defiance? What are we to make of the fact that since 1960 the population has increased by 41 percent but violent crime by 560 percent? The most active incubator for this violence is in the ten to seventeen age group, where the rate of the perpetration of violent crime has soared 400 percent since 1960. The killers of two-year-old James Bulger were in this age range. They abducted the toddler from a Liverpool shopping center and threw him in front of an onrushing train. Commenting at the time, Kenneth Baker (former United Kingdom home secretary) said: "When a young, innocent toddler is killed in a brutal way, then you are beyond the edge of evil; you are in the heart of darkness." Such darkness is terribly apparent in the swelling tide of high school killings. It is as though the very fabric of Western culture is unraveling before our eyes.

"It may be fairly claimed that [the story of Adam and Eve] gives the only convincing explanation of the perversity of human nature that the world has ever seen. Pascal said that the doctrine of original sin seems an offense to reason, but once accepted it makes total sense of the entire human condition."[1] This is in keeping with what we have already seen the Bible teaches us about the nature of human beings, namely, that we are not the product of some chance process and we clearly did not make ourselves. Instead, we have been made in the image of God with unique capacities (rationality, morality, the pursuit of beauty, fear of extinction, spiritual perception) which distinguish us from other life forms. But as we saw at the end of the last chapter, we are a paradox.

What do we mean by original sin? Interestingly, this is not a phrase we find in the Bible. It was coined apparently by our friend Augustine of Hippo. He might have invented the phrase, but the concept runs right through the Bible. It does not mean that sin is part of human nature as God made it. God made man upright and is not responsible for his crookedness (Ecclesiastes 7:29). Why, then, did the psalmist declare, "Surely I was sinful at birth, sinful from the time my mother conceived me" (Psalm 51:5)? He was not there describing a unique condition true only of himself. Rather, sinfulness marks everyone from birth. The underlying idea is this: We are not sinners because we sin, but rather we sin because we are sinners. As Alister McGrath puts it, the flaw in human nature is not acquired; it is inbuilt.[2] The reason for this is to be found in the fact that God made Adam, the first man, the representative for all his posterity. So when Adam defied God by eating the forbidden fruit, he took all of his descendants down with him. Just as a king involves his people in the consequence of his actions when he declares war, so Adam by eating of the Tree of the Knowledge of Good and Evil was essentially claiming that he could know and decide what was good and evil for him without consulting God. He involved all of humanity in the consequence of his actions.

Derek Prime tackles this "heavy" idea with a characteristic lightness of touch when he writes, "We inherit a sinful nature from our parents, as they did from theirs—a process which has gone on since man in the beginning rebelled against God. At birth we are full of the natural poison of sin (Matthew 15:11, 15–20; Mark 7:15, 20–23), similar to a newly hatched snake. This unhappy predicament provides no excuse for sins, but aggravates them. It is because we are sinners that we sin."[3] Man is not the victim of his environment. His troubles are in himself. As Cassius reminds Brutus in *Julius Caesar,* "The fault, dear Brutus, is not in the stars but in ourselves, that we are underlings." The environment in which God set Adam and Eve was perfect. It is sin that turns paradise into a wilderness.

By sin the New Testament means, not social error or failure in the first instance, but rebellion against, defiance of, retreat from and consequent guilt before, God the Creator; and sin, says the New Testament, is the basic evil from which we need deliverance, and from which Christ died to save us. All that has gone wrong in human life between man and man is ultimately due to sin, and our present state of being in the wrong with ourselves and our fellows cannot be cured as long as we remain in the wrong with God.[4]

Now, if we are tempted to veto this on the basis that it seems to imply, as Bruce Milne puts it, "an arbitrariness as far as our condemnation is concerned,"[5] we should keep in mind that when the Bible confronts the fact of our personal sinfulness, it points first to the way in which we as individuals fall short of God's standard. Once again, the apostle Paul helps us out. He is very clear about the fact of our solidarity with Adam: "Therefore, just as sin entered the world through one man, and death through sin, and in this way death came to all men, because all sinned" (Romans 5:12). But notice in his final phrase the fact of individual responsibility. Some verses earlier he had been driving this point home:

> Because of your stubbornness and your unrepentant heart, you are storing up wrath against yourself for the day of God's wrath, when his righteous judgment will be revealed. God "will give to each person according to what he has done." To those who by persistence in doing good seek glory, honor and immortality, he will give eternal life. But for those who are self-seeking and who reject the truth and follow evil, there will be wrath and anger. (Romans 2:5–8)

Now we should mention here something that we will expand on later, namely, that in the wonderful plan of God He has provided a Savior.

> *O loving mercy of our God,*
> *When all was sin and shame,*
> *A second Adam to the fight*
> *And for our rescue came.*

Perhaps you will be helped, as I have been, by thinking of it along these lines.[6] Original sin is that state into which we are born. Elsewhere this is described in terms of spiritual deadness. Consequently, we need to be "made alive." In other words, the doctrine of original sin basically affirms that we are born with a *need* to be born again. From birth I am estranged from God and therefore need to be reconciled. It is only when I am brought to recognize the *bad news* of my condition that I will begin to appreciate the *good news* of God's provision. But we're getting ahead of ourselves. We dare not advance to the cure until we have come to terms with the diagnosis.

Another question that almost inevitably arises when the discussion turns to the matter of sin is this: I have heard the phrase "total depravity" being used, and I wonder whether this means that each of us is as bad as we could possibly be?

The answer is no. What it does mean is that there is no part of our lives that is unaffected by sin no matter what part of our nature we care to reference. Our wills, emotions, minds, deeds, affections— *every* area—is touched and tainted by sin. Even the "good" things we do fail to measure up to the standard God has set. It is for this reason that nothing in us or about us gives us an edge with God. The heart of the human problem is the problem of the human heart. Genesis 6:5 tells us that prior to the flood, "The Lord saw how great man's wickedness on the earth had become, and that every inclination of the thoughts of his heart was only evil all the time." The words of Jesus to religious leaders who were consumed with cleanliness reinforce this truth that sin has affected the very core of the person.

> What comes out of a man is what makes him "unclean." For from within, out of men's hearts, come evil thoughts, sexual immorality, theft, murder, adultery, greed, malice, deceit, lewdness, envy, slander, arrogance and folly. All these evils come from inside and make a man "unclean." (Mark 7:20–23)

When we consider this statement in light of all the futile attempts to explain why men and women do the bad things they do, are we not at least willing to consider the possibility that here we have an explanation that actually fits the facts? In an earlier generation, T. H. Huxley summarized his perspective as follows: "The doctrines of the innate depravity of man appear to me to be vastly nearer the truth than the liberal popular illusions that all babies are born good, and that the example of a corrupt society is responsible for their failing to remain so."[7]

Surely nobody deep down believes that "education" is all that's necessary to tame the rebel, transform the liar, free the addict, and reconcile the warring gangs. That is why campaigns encouraging individuals to "Just Say No" are ultimately expressions of futility. Half the time the individual wants to say "Yes," and when she decides to say "No," she finds that she is incapable. It is because we are "totally depraved" in this biblical sense that we are utterly unable to save ourselves. Total depravity implies "total inability." So unless someone is able to effect a spiritual heart transplant, then our condition is hopeless. There is such a person, but that would be getting ahead of ourselves!

We have considered a couple of the hard questions regarding sin, but we haven't done enough to answer the essential question, What exactly is *sin?*

"Sin may be comprehensively defined as a lack of conformity to the law of God in act, habit, attitude, outlook, disposition, motivation, and mode of existence."[8]

It is surely not without significance that the very standard by which every life must be tested is banished from the halls of education and the courts of law and the corridors of power. We seem prepared to tolerate just about anything just so long as it makes no claims at truth, or worse still, may call us to account. Each of us, if we are honest, must confess that we fail to live up to even the standards we set for ourselves, let alone the standard set by God in the Ten Commandments. When these commandments are not simply disregarded, they tend to be thought of in much the same way as questions are to be answered in a college examination—five out of ten questions to be attempted.

Let's take the test.

1. Who takes first place?

"You shall have no other gods before me" (Exodus 20:3).

Can we honestly say that every day and in every way, it is God who is the exclusive object of our worship? Just in case we are tempted to water down the inherent demand, we should think of it in light of the words of Jesus. "Love the Lord your God with all your heart and with all your soul and with all your mind and with all your strength" (Mark 12:30; cf. Luke 10:25–28).

We break this command by seeking to dethrone God and put ourselves where He should be. We are too often self-made, and we inevitably worship our creator. It is in paganism that God exists for humans, rather than the other way around. When we are tempted to believe that by offering God something we can obligate Him to us, we are violating this command.

In his speech in Athens Paul was very clear: "[God] is not served by human hands, as if he needed anything, because he himself gives all men life and breath and everything else"(Acts 17:25). With our major universities offering courses in earth cults and feminine deities, we should not allow our ability at space exploration and computer technology to mask the fact that "we are anything but backward, unsophisticated neopagans who have drifted into superstition and foolishness."[9] When we ignore the prophet's warning against boasting about riches, physical strength, or intellectual achievement and choose to worship at the shrine marked "Self," we break this command.

2. What about those graven mistakes?

"You shall not make for yourself an idol in the form of anything in heaven above or on the earth beneath or in the waters below. You shall not bow down to them or worship them" (Exodus 20:4–5).

We do not have to be like the people in Athens, who had an elaborate system of shrines and idols, to violate this command. This has to do with the manner of our worship. What about all those occasions when we went through a "service of worship," and although our lips moved appropriately, our hearts were not engaged? The essence of idolatry (which this command forbids) is the entertainment of thoughts about God that are unworthy of Him. When, in the Old Testament, Aaron commissioned the fashioning of a golden calf as a visible symbol of the God who had brought the Israelites out of Egypt, he broke this commandment. If the bull was an attempt to portray God's power, it could not do so without denying God's purity. How could the glory and beauty of God's moral character be gathered from looking at the statue of a bull? The image obscured God's glory.

Packer points out that in fastening on the pathos of the Crucifixion by depicting Christ on the cross, we may portray Christ's suffering but in doing so obscure His victory, joy, and power. One of the reasons for creating "manageable" images of God is that we might have a god who is small enough to be grasped, weak enough to be manipulated, and soft enough not to punish wrongdoers. If the first command forbids the worship of any false God, here the second forbids the worship of the true God in a manner that is unworthy of Him.

3. What's in a name?

"You shall not misuse the name of the Lord your God, for the Lord will not hold anyone guiltless who misuses his name" (Exodus 20:7).

The name of God is precious. For the Jew it was regarded as too sacred to even take on their lips, and so they used the unpronounceable YHWH to describe God. When in the Psalms we read of the importance of remembering the name of the Lord our God, it is a reminder of the fact that God's name portrays His character. When Jesus referred to what He had done on earth, He said, speaking to the Father, "I have declared unto them thy name" (John 17:26 KJV). If the correct use of God's name demands reverence and reality, then we misuse His name when we are guilty of irreverence and unreality. We break this third commandment by perjury, blasphemy, and hypocrisy.

4. Holy day or holiday?

"Remember the Sabbath day by keeping it holy. Six days you shall labor and do all your work, but the

seventh day is a Sabbath to the Lord your God. On it
you shall not do any work" (Exodus 20:8–10).

Have we taken seriously the way in which God
has ordered the cycle of life so that our bodies and
minds receive the rest they require and our spirits
engage in the worship God prescribes? Do we
remember the Lord's Day? Or do we simply regard it
as an occasion to "please ourselves"? By this fourth
commandment God has provided the opportunity
to worship Him undisturbed by personal business
or pleasure. Should we not welcome such a day of
worship and service to God, uninterrupted by the
routine rush of work and recreation? When I disregard this day and choose to misuse it for selfish
ends, I am guilty of breaking God's law.

By now we have gone far enough to remove any
lingering notions we might have had about not being sinners. In fact, if we are honest, facing commandment number one should have taken care of it!
When we studied the Ten Commandments at Park-
side Church in 1993, one of the members came to
me after the third study to announce with shame
that he was, as he put it, 0 for 3. His honesty extended to saying that the best he felt he could hope for
was 1 for 9. He subsequently contacted me to acknowledge that his revised estimate was 0 for 10. In
considering these commands, it quickly becomes
apparent that we have broken God's law. When by
this means we are made aware of our sin, we may
find ourselves beginning to search for a Savior.

5. Family matters.

"Honor your father and your mother, so that you
may live long in the land the Lord your God is giving
you" (Exodus 20:12).

The well-being of a person, people, or nation begins in the home. Virtually all civilizations have regarded the recognition of parental authority as indispensable to a stable society. Parental authority is divinely delegated authority. Reverence for parents is an integral part of reverence for God. "You shall be holy, for I the Lord your God am holy. Every one of you shall revere his mother and his father" (Leviticus 19:2–3 NKJV). It should be no surprise that in a culture where God has become weightless there is such chaos and confusion within the home. When we deny our parents the respect they deserve, disobey their commands, refuse to be corrected by their discipline, and fail to repay the love, care, and trouble they have given us, we break this command.

6. Life is sacred.

"You shall not murder" (Exodus 20:13).

This sixth command is brief. It consists of only two words in Hebrew: *no murder.* The reference is to malicious or unlawful killing. While it is beyond our purpose here, we should note in passing that the Bible clearly distinguishes between murder, which is a crime, and the execution that may take place in punishment for murder (Romans 13:3–5; cf. 1 Peter 2:13–17). As we have seen, human life is sacred, first because it is God's gift, and second because man bears God's image. We honor God by respecting His image in each other, which means consistently preserving life and fostering each other's welfare. We break this command by homicide, suicide, abortion, and by the hidden murder of the heart by which we wish someone dead or when we kill them with our words. Just when we thought we had found one command that we were not guilty of breaking, it sneaks up and bites us! Just because we may not have shed human blood we are not necessarily guiltless. In light of Jesus' words, our malicious rumors, our cutting comments, and our looks which could kill all serve to prove how guilty we are.

7. Whom God has joined together . . .

"You shall not commit adultery" (Exodus 20:14).

The Bible makes clear that in marriage, a man and a woman do not simply form a convenient contractual relationship. They enter into a covenant. They become one. The sexual union is the clearest indication that in marriage one plus one equals one. This union is so sacred that it is not to be intruded upon nor arbitrarily broken up. These five simple words of command condemn every conceivable way in which we contrive to abuse the sacred beauty of sex as placed by God within (and only within) the bonds of marriage. Jesus closed the loopholes we thought we had found when He informed His listeners that anyone who looks lustfully at a woman has in his heart already broken the marriage vow! In committing adultery, we sin against God, our body, the partner in the affair, our spouse, and our partner's spouse.

8. I was only borrowing it!

"You shall not steal" (Exodus 20:15).

I read recently of a schoolteacher who, in seeking to impress upon her class the importance of honesty, asked the question, "Suppose you found a briefcase with half a million dollars in it. What would you do?" One boy raised his hand immediately and replied, "If it belonged to a poor family I'd return it!" Here, as elsewhere, the relativistic ethic which pervades our culture becomes apparent. It is not uncommon to hear the "Robin Hood" principle trotted out in defense of theft from institutions or "the rich." To steal from another is to sin against that person and against God. By taking what is not ours to have, we harm him, disregard him, and devalue him. Whenever I borrow and fail to return, when I am able to clear myself of debt and fail to do so, when I misuse my employer's time or property, when I cheat in the classroom or in the bedroom, when I ruin the reputation of another by slander, then I break this command.

> Good name in man and woman, dear my lord,
> Is the immediate jewel of their souls:
> Who steals my purse, steals trash; 'tis something, nothing;
> 'Twas mine, 'tis his, and has been slave to thousands;
> But he that filches from me my good name
> Robs me of that which not enriches him
> And makes me poor indeed.
>
> (*Othello* 3.30155–61)

9. The truth matters.

"You shall not give false testimony against your neighbor" (Exodus 20:16).

According to the research data for *The Day America Told the Truth*,[10] Americans lie. They lie more than we had ever thought possible before the study. Apparently just about everyone lies: 91 percent of us lie regularly. The majority of us find it hard to get through a week without lying. One in five can't make it through a single day—and we're talking about conscious, premeditated lies. When we refrain from lying, it's less often because we think it's wrong (only 45 percent) than for a variety of other reasons, among them the fear of being caught (17 percent). The report states that lying has become a cultural trait in America; it is embedded in our national character. Furthermore, the majority of Americans today (two out of three) believe there is nothing wrong with telling a lie. Only 31 percent of us believe honesty is the best policy.

Once again, there is a direct relationship between the way in which people view the world and the way in which they live their lives. When an individual believes that truth is relative and not absolute, then he cannot *know* the truth; and if truth is only what you subjectively think, how can you *tell* the truth? In direct contrast, the Bible declares that God is a truth-telling, promise-keeping God who "cannot lie," and He is described as hating lies and deception. This certainly addresses the question of perjury, but it doesn't end there. When we fail to speak in defense of a friend, when we distort the truth by our exaggerations, or when we are slanderous, then we are brought face-to-face with the fact of our sinfulness.

10. The other man's grass.

"You shall not covet your neighbor's house. You shall not covet your neighbor's wife, or his manservant or maidservant, his ox or donkey, or anything that belongs to your neighbor" (Exodus 20:17).

Living, as we do, in a culture that encourages one-upmanship, we are going to be hard-pressed to convince ourselves (we certainly will be unable to convince anyone else, not least of all God) that we are free of guilt in this regard. This commandment gets to the heart of the matter insofar as it addresses our inner life. Here, in the realm of our thinking, where others cannot go, we are without excuse before God, who searches our hearts. Coveting conveys the thought of seeking dishonest and dishonorable gain. The apostle Paul refers to it as idolatry because the things we covet become our god, controlling our lives (Colossians 3:5).

There is a real sense in which coveting may be regarded as the root of all social evils. When I cultivate desires that are out of control, then I am bound to produce actions to match. For example, when David coveted Bathsheba, he broke the tenth commandment. When he took her, he broke the eighth. When he slept with her, he broke the seventh, and when he arranged for her husband to be killed, he broke the sixth. But it all began with covetousness. Learning to be content with what we have is a safeguard against the temptation to break the previous nine commands.

For some, this material will have been very familiar and you have moved through it quickly. Others may have been struck for the first time by the extent to which your life is marked by patterns of sinful behavior. Now it starts to make sense when sin is described in terms of "missing the mark." If this is the standard, then honesty demands that I recognize myself to have missed it. Until now, we have been content to establish our own standards of righteousness. This has afforded us the luxury of being able to change the rules to accommodate our imperfections. But before God we cannot be successful. We can run, but ultimately we cannot hide.

What we have to face is the fact that we have offended God. We have shaken our fist in His face. We have put ourselves in the wrong with Him, and the gravest aspect in all of this is not found in the effect it has upon me, nor on others, but primarily upon God. If we consider our sin only by comparing it with what others have done, then we will find some basis for excuse or even congratulation ("Well, at least I'm not a serial killer"). But when we understand that God is so holy and pure that He cannot look on evil and wrongdoing; that His inevitable and settled reaction to sin is anger; then we will either determine that we must run for cover or come out with our hands up and admit that our predicament is such that we are clearly unable to extricate ourselves.

This, then, is the explanation for the sense of alienation that you feel. Not just from God, or even others, but from yourself. This is why it always seems that there is a piece missing from the jigsaw of your life. There is a loss of clear direction, a sense of ambiguity, and a whole army of conflicting desires that jumble up your mind. This explains the bondage you feel to patterns of wrong behavior; and now you begin to grasp the reason for the conflict that exists between yourself and others.

Perhaps the biggest temptation at this point on the journey is to run and try to find a substitute god who will not draw us out into the light and expose our guilt. There are plenty of available scarecrows in the melon patch, as we have seen. But remember, they may have ears, but they cannot hear; and eyes, but they cannot see. They are worse than useless.

As painful as this diagnosis may be, if you acknowledge its accuracy, then you should take hope because, as Jesus explained to the people of His day, it is only the sick who go to the doctor. He did not come to call people who were sure of their own well-being; He came to call sinners to repentance. The fact is this: God makes us realize how ill we are before He makes us better.

When the apostle Paul introduced the need for repentance (a change of heart, mind, and direction), he introduced the fact that the effects of sin go beyond this life. "[God] has set a day when he will judge the world with justice by the man he has appointed. He has given proof of this to all men by raising him from the dead" (Acts 17:31). It is time for us to look more closely at Jesus and particularly the significance of His death and the fact of His resurrection.

We have learned that the Bible makes clear that mankind is marked by paradox. First, we are creatures of God, made in His image and therefore with a measure of dignity. Second, that we are sinners, living in rebellion and marked by depravity. Pascal combined these truths when he spoke of man as a dethroned monarch, cast down from his former eminence, vanquished and depraved, yet never quite able to forget what he once was and hence ought to be.[11] This biblical explanation that affirms our having been made not only *by* God but *for* Him provides us with the only convincing explanation of the perversity of human nature. Unlike other anthropologies, the Christian view makes total sense of the entire human condition.

4

The Big Picture

Most of us have either seen or played the quiz game where one small section of a photograph is displayed as a hint of the larger scene from which it has been taken. We are then left to try and figure out what the bigger picture is. It quickly becomes apparent that it is possible to jump to all kinds of faulty conclusions. It is only when the total scene is revealed that confusion gives way to clarity.

By now it should be apparent that I am suggesting that if we are going to make sense of the various elements of Christianity we must view them in light of the "big picture." For example, if I make the bold declaration, "Christ is the answer," I ought not to be surprised if your rejoinder proves to be, "What is the question?" Imagine someone walking up Main Street and accosting people with the statement: "The answer is 1066." She would receive all kinds of reactions, and her information would prove helpful only to whoever happened to be on Main Street desperately concerned to find an answer to the question, "When was the Battle of Hastings?" Clearly there is a vast difference in the significance of the two events. I could safely argue that knowledge of the date of some eleventh-century battle is largely irrelevant. However, I would want to argue for the pressing, immediate relevance of the Christian faith. But in order to do so, I cannot assume that you will have the background information which allows you to agree with my assertion. In the same way that it is important to keep looking at the big picture when one is completing a jigsaw puzzle, we begin to understand how the "pieces" of Christianity fit together by viewing them in light of a biblical worldview.

Here is what I mean. We can summarize in four words the way in which the Bible views the span of history: *creation, fall, redemption, consummation.* Since one of the charges which is brought against Christians is that in attempting to explain ourselves we use far too many, largely incomprehensible, nouns which end in "-tion," let me immediately use four other, more accessible words: *good, bad, new, perfect.*

Good is, as we have seen, how the Bible describes God's creative handiwork. "God saw all that he had made, and it was very good" (Genesis 1:31). Along with the privileges man enjoys come the responsibilities. It is here in the biblical teaching about Creation that the basis for these obligations is established.

Bad is, as we have also seen, the way in which the Bible depicts our dilemma. Both by nature and by choice we are rebels. Instead of enjoying His company, we turn our backs on Him. We are not prepared to do the one thing He asks of us (Genesis 2:16–17). So we find ourselves alienated, living with a sense of shame; and the sorry implications of our behavior become apparent in our condition. We are deceived and justly condemned and "without hope and without God in the world" (Ephesians 2:12).

The story, as we will see, ends with the *perfect*. We will come to that. For now, Fellini's expression of despair brings us appropriately to consider what we mean when we refer to the *new*. Let's go back to our friends in Athens to get some help with this. Remember, the city was full of idols. The Athenians had developed quite an assortment of worship locations which acted as potential points of contact with God. But the very fact that they had an altar that bore the inscription "TO AN UNKNOWN GOD" (Acts 17:23) lets us see that by their own ingenious searching, they were unable to close the gap. The predicament is not limited to *there* and *then;* if we are honest, we face it in the *here* and *now*. One of the sorry implications of our rebellion or indifference toward God is simply this: we cannot know Him. He is beyond the ability of our minds to conceive and, worse still, "His purity shrivels our endemic human wickedness."[1]

Now here is where the Good News comes in. God decided to take the initiative in approaching us. We have noted the Bible's claim that God created the world. We should therefore not be surprised that creation points to Him. "The heavens declare the glory of God; the skies proclaim the work of his hands" (Psalm 19:1). In the same psalm we read of the laws that govern the movement of the sun. Our world is full of the evidence of intelligent design. God has ordered things in such a way that it would cause men and women to seek Him, to reach out for Him (Acts 17:27). It is on account of this that as human beings we are prompted to ask questions about the world. And there is, as McGrath points out, something about the world that allows answers to those questions to be given. John Polkinghorne, who was professor of mathematical physics at the University of Cambridge, points out that in order for the universe to emerge as it did, a whole series of interconnected conditions had to be in place. "There is a delicate and intricate balance in its structure necessary for the emergence of life. For example, suppose things had been a little different in those crucial first three minutes when the gross nuclear structure of the world got fixed as a quarter helium and three-quarters hydrogen. If things had gone a little faster, all would have been helium; and without hydrogen how could water (vital to life) have been able to form?"[2]

This is essentially the reasoning we discover in Aquinas's "Five Ways," five arguments which suggest that the Christian belief in God is perfectly consistent with the world as we know it.

1. Aquinas observed that things are moving. Our world is dynamic. Things are in a constant state of flux. How is it that nature is in motion? Things don't just move by themselves; they are moved by something else. Imagine one of those displays of dominoes toppling each other down. Each one is caused to fall by the motion of the previous domino. But when we trace the domino effect back to its source, we discover a hand toppling the first domino. This was Aquinas's argument. There are a whole series of causes of motion lying behind the world. Unless there is an infinite number of

these causes, then there must be a single cause right at the origin of the series. And from this original cause, all other motion is ultimately derived. This original cause, argues Aquinas, this "unmoved mover," is God Himself.

2. The second way is based on the existence of cause and effect in the world. Reasoning as he did in relation to motion, Aquinas argued that all effects may be traced to an original cause—which is God Himself.

3. The third way is not so immediately obvious. Aquinas noted that the world contains beings (such as ourselves) which aren't there by necessity. This is in distinct contrast to God, who is a *necessary* being. The fact that we are here demands an explanation. One being is brought into existence by another being which already exists. When we trace this series of causes back to the original cause, it can only be someone whose existence is necessary—in other words—God.

4. The fourth way argues that human values such as honesty, goodness, and dignity must emerge from something which is in itself true and good and noble. The origin of each of these, says Aquinas, is God, who is their original cause.

5. The fifth way is the argument from design. In the same way that when you arrive home and find the table set for a meal you recognize that the silverware and china have not arrived by chance but by design, so too in the natural ordering of our world, we see the hand of God.

Although these arguments are often referred to as "proofs for the existence of God," Alister McGrath points out that this is not correct.

On the basis of these considerations, Aquinas concludes that it is rational to believe in God. Not for one
moment does he suggest that these constitute *proofs*
for the existence of God, as if they provided some
kind of knock- down argument for the reality of God.
Rather, he is concerned to demonstrate that reason is
capable of pointing in the direction of God, and lend-
ing its support to those who already believe in Him.[3]

So "creation is like a signpost, pointing away
from itself to its creator." As we shall see, consideration or even acceptance of this fact is not sufficient
for us to find and know God. We need to follow
where the signpost leads. In his sermon, Paul moves
quickly to the resurrection of Jesus Christ. If his listeners are interested in proof that the view of the
world which he has been expounding is true, then
they will find it in the fact of the Resurrection. Interestingly, Polkinghorne recognizes that the signpost
of creation may incline an individual to take a "the-
istic view" of the world. But he goes on: "By themselves that is about as far as they would get me. The
reason why I take my stand within the Christian
community lies in certain events which took place in
Palestine nearly two thousand years ago."[4]

He is referring, of course, to the life, death, and
resurrection of Jesus of Nazareth. Now it is this
matter of the resurrection of Jesus which Paul
introduces and which causes the interruption that
essentially concludes his talk. Why would he begin
with what is essentially "the end of the story"?
Some of his other writings help us to answer that.
For example, when he wrote to the members of the
church in Corinth, he made it clear that if the Resurrection is not historically true, then Christianity

collapses immediately. "If Christ has not been raised, our preaching is useless and so is your faith" (1 Corinthians 15:14). We should note, in passing, that this is one of the distinctive features of the Christian faith. Other religions, whether Islam or Buddhism, do not rely on the continued living presence of their founder as the basis for their claims to truth. But Christianity cannot get away so easily. Listen again to Paul, "And if Christ has not been raised, your faith is futile; you are still in your sins" (v. 17).

On a very personal level, Paul had every reason to begin with this pivotal event of human history. After all, the early chapters of his life were marked not simply by disinterest toward Jesus but by outright animosity. If you have never read the story of Paul's conversion, you can find it recorded in chapter 9 of Acts. Let me summarize the event by paraphrasing his own account when he was called before King Agrippa (Acts 26).

My accusers can tell you as well as I can that from the time I was a child I was totally committed to Judaism. I was born in Tarsus of Cilicia but brought up in Jerusalem. I had Gamaliel as my teacher— probably the best there was at that time. Whether you consider my family tree, my orthodoxy in belief and practice, or my zealous interest in persecuting the Christians—I was endeavoring to literally destroy the church—my record speaks for itself. Ironically, it is because I believe that God has fulfilled the promises He made to my forefathers that I am on trial today. In other words, far from my being involved in some newfangled, upstart religion, I have discovered in the "second half of the story" what it is that my people are hoping for, as they continue to serve God sincerely and continuously.

There is really no reason why any of the Pharisees who are accusing me should find it incredible that God raises the dead. They know that even our father Abraham, when he was called on to sacrifice his son Isaac, proceeded to do as he was told because he figured that God was certainly able to raise the dead. So for me to be hauled in here because of my hope in the Resurrection is really a bit much!

Now you are probably wondering just how it was that I went from persecuting the followers of Jesus to actually becoming one of them. It is totally incredible to me even now, as I think about it. I realize that it was God's plan, from before the beginning of time, to call me by His grace and use me to let people like you know that His Son, Jesus, really is alive.

Well, in Jerusalem, with the assistance of the chief priests, I saw to it that as many as possible of these "Christians" were put in prison. I did not care whether they were men or women. All I needed to know was that they were following Christ, and then I struck with chilling vengeance. When a number of them were summarily executed, I was involved in making that happen. I made it my practice to go around the synagogues where they were gathering and do everything I could to make them blaspheme. In the process, I saw to it that they were soundly punished. I had such an insatiable desire to destroy these people that I even began traveling to foreign cities to find them and subject them to the same kind of abuse I had been meting out in Jerusalem.

It was actually when I was on one of these journeys that this amazing event took place. I was with some companions, and we were heading for Damascus. It

was right around lunchtime when our party was quite
literally engulfed in a light from heaven that was even
brighter than the sun. One minute we were proceeding
as normal and the next we were biting the dust. Then I
heard a voice calling me by name and confronting me:
"Why do you persecute Me?" I remember thinking,
This is bizarre. After all, I wasn't persecuting a person. I was chasing down as many people as I could
get my hands on. Still not quite sure just what was
happening, I ventured a reply: "Who are you?" And
then it suddenly struck me—He is Lord! "I am Jesus
whom you are persecuting."

   This, as you would imagine, is the last thing in the
world I would have expected. Everything in me believed, and wanted to believe, that this Jesus of
Nazareth had come to a sorry end—and that all His
outlandish claims had been laid to rest with Him in a
Palestinian tomb. It wasn't as if I were somehow predisposed to belief. In fact, if they had conducted a
survey to find the man least likely to believe that Jesus
is alive, there is no doubt that I would have been at
the top of the list.

   Right then and there, the risen Christ commissioned me for service. I was, He told me, to embark
on a mission that would see men and women discover forgiveness for their sins and all that goes with that
life-changing experience. So, that's what I have been
doing; and believe me, all that I am saying is just
what Moses and our prophets were saying in their
day.

   I know, King Agrippa, that you are aware of these
things, and I'm pretty sure that you believe what the
prophets were saying when they predicted that the
Messiah would be silent before His accusers and

would be assigned a grave with the wicked and with the rich in His death.

"Do you really think that you can in such a short time convince me to become a Christian?"

Yes, King Agrippa. Short time or long, it is my earnest prayer that not only you, but the rest who are listening to this, will discover forgiveness and freedom in the Lord Jesus. In short, that you may become like me—apart from these chains, of course!

What are we to make of this? Was Festus right when he interrupted Paul and shouted, "You are out of your mind, Paul! . . . Your great learning is driving you insane" (Acts 26:24). It is not unusual to hear the resurrection of Jesus dismissed as simply some sort of wish fulfillment on the part of the disciples. But why would they have responded to the catastrophe of Jesus' death by making the unprecedented suggestion that He had been raised from the dead? Even if that were to have been true of those men on account of their devotion, it would provide no explanation for the self-confessed transformation in the thinking and acting of Saul of Tarsus. What, we must ask, is the most plausible and probable explanation of the historical evidence? It will not do to reason as follows: (1) Dead people do not rise from the dead. (2) Therefore, Jesus Christ did not rise from the dead. (3) Subject closed. In this approach the conclusion is drawn from the premise without any consideration of the evidence. Unfortunately, it would seem that it is not uncommon for men and women to have rejected Christianity, not because they examined the claims and found them unimpressive, but because they left them unexamined. That this is true when it comes to the evidence for the Resurrection can scarcely be doubted. In talking with friends who are unashamed members of "Agnostics Anonymous," I often begin at this point. There are all kinds of questions about the nature of Christianity which present themselves to the thoughtful mind. We can consider them as they surface, but this issue of the Resurrection towers like a colossus over every other consideration. Dispense with the Resurrection and the Christian faith is, as we have seen (1 Corinthians 15:14), emptied of all content and value. This is probably why, over the years, it has been subjected to such a barrage of sustained criticism.

But even secular historians refer to the person of Christ and to the actions of His followers. Tacitus, a Roman historian, provides a careful year-by-year account of the early days of the Roman Empire. In describing the events of A.D. 64 he acknowledges that Nero was responsible for the fire of Rome. He wanted to redevelop a large area in the city as his palace.

> To dispel this rumor, Nero substituted as culprits and treated with the most extreme punishment some people, popularly known as Christians, whose disgraceful activities were notorious. [They were accused, for example, of cannibalism on the strength of their celebration of the Lord's Supper.] The originator of the name, Christ, had been executed when Tiberius was emperor by order of the procurator Pontius Pilate. But the deadly cult, though checked for a time, was now breaking out again not only in Judea, the birthplace of this evil, but even throughout Rome, where all nasty and disgusting ideas from all over the world pour in and find a ready following. (Tacitus *Annals* 15.44)

One of Tacitus's contemporaries was a man called Pliny the Younger, who, in A.D. 112, became governor of Bithynia in northern Turkey. In the course of sending reports to the emperor, Trajan, he wrote a long letter about Christians in which he made clear that they were becoming the source of economic and social problems. The pagan festivals were not being so well attended, the temples were losing numbers, and the revenue from the sale of sacrificial animals was drying up. Pliny was honest enough to point out that these Christians were living exemplary lives and their whole guilt lay in the fact that they refused to worship the imperial statue and images of the gods. They insisted on meeting on a fixed day, Sunday, and at those gatherings they sang hymns to Christ as God.

What made them intolerable was their insistence that Jesus must not be regarded as simply an addition to the Roman pantheon. No, for them Jesus was Lord, and before His name every knee was one day going to bow. And what had been the catalyst for them to live and die with such conviction? The fact that they were in absolutely no doubt that He had risen from the grave, just as He had promised He would. In other words, the *fact* of the Resurrection was the basis of the *faith* of the disciples. To suggest, as some do, that the Easter fact derived from the Easter faith of the disciples is to fail to deal adequately with the evidence. "The circumstances in which Jesus died render this interpretation utterly fanciful."[5]

JESUS WAS DEAD

It is important that the fact of His death be verified. There have been those who have argued that

Jesus was never actually dead; and so after He had "come around" in the tomb, He managed to persuade His followers of His resurrection. This will not do. If there was one thing for which these particular soldiers were known, it was their ability to carry out executions. "You did not survive a Roman crucifixion: they were experts at this macabre form of execution."[6] Just for the record, we have the eyewitness news from John. He tells us that the Jews did not want the bodies left on the crosses during the Sabbath. The soldiers were dispatched by Pilate to break the legs of the victims and, by doing so, hasten their deaths. Having broken the legs of two of the men, they turned their attention to Jesus. And here we have this fascinating piece of testimony from John: "But when they came to Jesus and found that *he was already dead,* they did not break his legs. Instead, one of the soldiers pierced Jesus' side with a spear, bringing a sudden flow of blood and water" (John 19:33–34, italics added). Without knowing it, the writer provides evidence of one of the strongest proofs of death—the separation of the dark clot from the clear serum. In the practicalities which follow, nobody involved, whether governor, centurion, friend, or embalmer, appears to be in any doubt about whether Jesus was really dead.

THE TOMB WAS EMPTY

"On the first day of the week, very early in the morning, the women took the spices they had prepared and went to the tomb. They found the stone rolled away from the tomb, but when they entered, they did not find the body of the Lord Jesus" (Luke 24:1–3).

These words from Luke concur with the other three Gospels. By Easter Sunday morning, the body was gone. The fact is not in dispute. The question is how to explain it.

Throughout the years, a number of explanations have come in and out of fashion. It has been suggested that the reason the women found the tomb empty was because they were at the wrong tomb! This will not do. First of all, they were sensible women. There is nothing about their approach that speaks of anything other than the most practical expressions of care and devotion. At least two of them were aware of the location of the burial, and even if they had arrived mistakenly at the wrong place, they would have quickly rectified their error. They could have checked with Joseph, who surely was not about to make the same mistake. He had personally been responsible for placing Jesus' body in "his own new tomb that he had cut out of the rock" (Matthew 27:60).

And what about the notion that the enemies of Jesus stole the body? Why? It is hard to imagine just what their motive might have been. After all, they had been working hard to bring about His death, and they were very concerned to make sure that He stayed where He had been put! The concern of the chief priests and Pharisees was to ensure that none of Jesus' friends took the body. They had no reason to want Him anywhere else than in the tomb. Here is how they put their request to Pilate for security:

> "Sir," they said, "we remember that while he was still alive that deceiver said, 'After three days I will rise again.' So give the order for the tomb to be made

secure until the third day. Otherwise, his disciples may come and steal the body and tell the people that he has been raised from the dead. This last deception will be worse than the first." (Matthew 27:63–64)

Are we then to believe that it was actually the friends of Jesus who stole the body? How did they get past the well-trained guard of Roman soldiers? Who moved the stone? Why did they then take the time to remove the grave clothes and leave them looking so untouched? Could it be that they were successful in manhandling this dead body into some other place of seclusion without giving anybody an inkling of what was happening? The soldiers were paid to offer the feeble explanation that this had taken place while they were asleep. All of the soldiers asleep? And if they were asleep, how were they able to give a credible report of what had happened?

But let's suppose, for the sake of argument, that the disciples had actually stolen the body. We are then forced to conclude that when they hit the streets of Jerusalem with their message, *Jesus is alive!* they were lying through their teeth. This just isn't plausible. The gospel writers are brutally honest about the response of His followers to His death. Frightened that they might be next in line, they ran for safety, thoroughly disappointed that all their hopes and dreams had fizzled out in the sorry spectacle of the Crucifixion. John describes the scene on the evening of the first day of the week. The disciples were together, but they were not on the streets proclaiming Jesus. They were behind closed and locked doors *for fear of the Jews* (John 20:19). So we are asked to believe that, perhaps because they felt

guilty about their cowardly performance, they managed to muster up enough courage to steal the body
and parlay this fraud into a religious movement. It
would be one thing to believe this if they were to
benefit in any way from the lie. But the record
shows that they were hounded, despised, persecut-
ed, and killed for maintaining that what they knew
to be a lie was actually true. "If they had themselves
taken the body of Jesus, to preach His resurrection
was to spread a known, planned falsehood. They not
only preached it; they suffered for it. They were prepared to go to prison, to the flogging post, and to
death for a fairy-tale. This simply does not ring true."[7]
As John Blanchard states, "Men may be prepared to
die for a conviction but not for a concoction!"

Perhaps we can pause for a moment to recognize
how relevant these considerations are at a time
when there is such a growing interest in "Unsolved
Mysteries." One is tempted to suggest, in light of
some of the more bizarre investigations today, that
the greatest unsolved mystery is why anyone would
ever pay attention to such far-fetched tales! However, quite frequently the "mystery" is related to
"near-death experiences." In each case, the person
has not died, but in coming very near to death has
reported perceptions of what seems to happen close
to death.

Well, in Jesus we are dealing with someone who,
as we have already noted, really died. What's more,
He has returned from the dead and provides us
with indications of what we might anticipate. In the
gospel records we find the claims, not of a fallible
Shirley MacLaine, but of One who has died and has
been raised from the dead and is able to give a first-
hand account of transcendent spiritual realities. So

for those who are concerned about the New Age discussions of "transcendent knowing," let me encourage you to think this through. And when that search includes a willingness to explore the realm and role of angels, you will discover plenty here for you to ponder. In thinking along these lines, we would be irresponsible if we did not take time to consider . . .

THE UNDISTURBED GRAVE CLOTHES

At the end of the nineteenth chapter of John's gospel we have the account of two men (Joseph of Arimathea and Nicodemus) embalming the body of Jesus with a mixture of myrrh and aloes, some seventy-five pounds. "Taking Jesus' body, the two of them wrapped it, with the spices, in strips of linen. This was in accordance with Jewish burial customs" (John 19:40). The final phrase is a reminder to us that everything was being done "by the book."

Now, when the disciples, in response to the report of the women, ran to the tomb, it is clear that they were startled, not only by the absence of the body of Jesus, but also by the condition of the grave clothes. It is clear from the description that these were not found lying like a stack of laundry in a disheveled heap. It would appear that they were intact. The distance preserved between the body cloths and the head napkin was enough, in accordance with oriental custom, that his face and neck would have been bare. While it would appear that the body cloths were lying flat, presumably having given way to the weight of the spices, the word which is used to describe the condition of the head napkin might be translated "twirled." The picture, then, would be of a kind of crumpled turban that even without a head inside had retained its shape on account of the crisscross pattern of the strips of burial cloth. How do we account for such a phenomenon?

The answer lies in the nature of what had taken place in the Resurrection. We are wrong to imagine Jesus "kind of waking up" and beginning to pick away at the bandages. For one thing, it would have been impossible for Him to make much use of his arms, given the weight of the spices. When Lazarus had been resuscitated (you can read the story in John 11), he emerged from the grave in need of assistance to be freed of the burial cloths. The resurrection of Jesus was clearly vastly different. He passed miraculously from death into a totally new sphere of existence. This becomes apparent in some of His appearances when He passes through closed doors. Without entering into speculative fancies about the "fourth dimension," we should nevertheless recognize that the reason for the undisturbed grave clothes is to be found in the fact that His body was transmuted into something new (while retaining aspects of the old) and unbelievably wonderful. If we had been present to see it happen, we would not have seen it happen! One moment the body would have been lying dead, and then we would have been aware of the fact that it had gone—we might say *vaporized!*

Here is material to stretch the minds of all the sci-fi buffs. Indeed, far more staggering ideas than these are accepted with ease by science fiction aficionados. Why men and women swallow Von Daniken while choking on the claims of Scripture is explained by Paul when he writes to the church in Corinth: "The god of this age has blinded the minds of unbelievers, so that they cannot see the light of the gospel of the glory of Christ, who is the image of God" (2 Corinthians 4:4).

This is a necessary and timely reminder of the fact that the "arguments" I am presenting in defense of the Christian faith are insufficient in and of themselves to move the reader from unbelief to certainty, from doubt to faith. It would be unbearable to think that such transformations rested upon one's ability to use the right words in the proper order to the best effect. However, it may be (please, God) that He will choose on account of His grace to use the very weakness and familiarity of our words and arguments in the process of gentle divine persuasion. Such a process whereby the Holy Spirit applies words to our minds and causes faith to be born of understanding is, according to the shorter Scottish catechism, "the work of God's Spirit whereby, convincing us of our sin and misery, enlightening our minds in the knowledge of Christ, and renewing our wills, he doth persuade and enable us to embrace Jesus Christ freely offered to us in the gospel."[8]

John tells us that when the disciples had gone back to their homes, Mary had another look into the tomb. She saw two angels sitting where Jesus' body had been, and they inquired of her just why she was crying. It was going to take a personal encounter with the risen Jesus to answer her questions, dry her tears, and transform her life.

JESUS APPEARED

If all that we had by way of evidence was an empty tomb, then it would be possible to explain it away. Instead, we discover that over a period of some six weeks Jesus appeared to different people in a variety of situations. The suggestion that these "appearances" can be dismissed as nothing more than inventions or hallucinations does not stand up to honest scrutiny. A hallucination is the "apparent perception of an external object when no such object is present." For example, in the famous dagger scene in *Macbeth*, the king says, "Is this a dagger which I see before me, the handle toward my hand? Come, let me clutch thee. I have thee not, and yet I see thee still" (*Macbeth* 2.1.33–35). In this case, the mind of Macbeth was filled with all kinds of predispositions. This is characteristic of hallucinatory behavior. It is associated with periods of exaggerated wishful thinking or, as in Macbeth's case, overwhelming guilt. At the same time, hallucinations occur when the circumstances are favorable. Now, when we examine the appearances of Jesus, we find that they are not marked by external circumstances that are predisposing or by strong convictions on the part of the individuals to believe that Jesus was alive. Let me encourage you to read the accounts of the various appearances. I think you will be struck by their diversity: a variety of people, in a variety of places, and in each case doing and presumably feeling different things.

For example, when the women returned from the empty tomb to tell the disciples what they had (or if you like, had not) seen, Luke is honest enough to record the fact that far from jumping on some wish fulfillment bandwagon, the disciples were skeptical: "But they did not believe the women, because their words seemed to them like nonsense" (Luke 24:11). Later on, when two of the disciples were on their way to Emmaus, they were so convinced of the fact that Jesus was dead and gone that they failed to recognize Him until they ate together. "Then their eyes were opened and they recognized him, and he disappeared from their sight" (Luke 24:31). So you see, it was not that they were expecting the risen Christ; nothing could have been further from their minds.

The classic illustration is of course that of the individual whom we have come to refer to as "doubting Thomas." Jesus had appeared to the group when Thomas was absent. When the others told him that they had seen the Lord, he was stubborn in his refusal to accept their testimony at face value. "Unless I see the nail marks in his hands and put my finger where the nails were, and put my hand into his side, I will not believe it" (John 20:25). I think you would agree that those are not the words of a man with a predisposition to believe. What, then, is it that brings about the transformation in Thomas and the others?

CHANGED LIVES

We have mentioned this in passing, and we need to give it the attention it deserves. Remember where we find them immediately following these dramatic events. Again, John is honest enough to admit, "On the evening of that first day of the week, when the disciples were together, with the doors locked for fear of the Jews" (John 20:19). Now look at what they are doing within a matter of weeks. They are filling Jerusalem with the news that "the God of our fathers raised Jesus from the dead" (Acts 5:30). Neither threats, nor beatings, nor imprisonment can prevent them from hazarding their lives for the sake of this story.

The drama is striking in the life of Simon Peter. He had gone into hiding with the others, and with plenty to think about. Despite his bold affirmations and strong convictions, he had come apart at the seams when Christ was arrested. Confronted by the questions of a servant girl, he had vehemently denied any knowledge of Christ. Only the bitterness of his remorseful tears could match the intensity with which he had cursed and sworn in disavowing allegiance to Jesus (Mark 14:66–72). Then, as we turn a few pages, we find him on the streets of Jerusalem defying the authorities as he explained with a new boldness, "God raised him from the dead, freeing him from the agony of death, because it was impossible for death to keep its hold on him" (Acts 2:24). And despite the attempts of the religious authorities to silence them and prevent the spread of this movement, Peter and John spoke for the rest of them when they declared, "We cannot help speaking about what we have seen and heard" (4:20).

And the change in peoples' lives did not stop in the first century, nor has it been limited by geography. We could fill this book and many more with the stories of those whose lives have been changed and who do not simply claim that Jesus rose from the dead but that He is alive today and that they know Him and communicate with Him. It is hard to come up with a credible explanation for the empty tomb, the appearances, the changed lives, and, as we shall see, the existence of the church, other than the fact that the Resurrection was a space-time occurrence in history.

THE CHURCH WAS BORN

"Without the Resurrection there simply would have been no Christian community to uphold and proclaim the gospel over twenty centuries."[9] Now do not get sidetracked by thinking immediately of dilapidated buildings and dwindling congregations. We are referring to the enthusiastic three thousand who responded to Peter's sermon and whose lives were vibrant expressions of the reality of forgiveness and the joyful anticipation of heaven and the present experience of peace and purpose. The church is made up of those in every generation whose lives have been transformed by the power of a risen Savior. This vast company transcends racial, economic, social, and national boundaries. How do we explain its beginning, let alone its spectacular growth? If you think about it, the early Christians were, in some ways, fairly indistinguishable from orthodox Jews. They tended to gather at the synagogues and, as they did, they expressed their conviction that Jesus was the One of whom the prophets had written. He was the long-awaited Messiah, who had by His resurrection demonstrated His victory over death and, as we shall see, indicated His divine identity. Three major changes are, I suggest, understandable only on account of the Resurrection.

Baptism

It is not that there was no baptism prior to the emergence of the church. There clearly were all kinds of washings in the Old Testament, the intertestamental period, and in the activities of John the Baptist. What was so obviously different was the significance which was attached to the event. These initial believers in Jesus were, in going down into the water, identifying with Christ in His death. And as they emerged from the water, they were united with Him in His resurrection. They came to see in baptism a picture of death and resurrection. "We were therefore buried with him through baptism into death in order that, just as Christ was raised from the dead through the glory of the Father, we too may live a new life" (Romans 6:4).

Holy Communion

As these new believers began to do what Jesus had instructed, they were looking back to His death on their behalf and looking forward in expectation of heaven. From the very start, the disciples began to devote themselves to "the breaking of bread" (Acts 2:42). This was in obedience to Christ's command. Paul explained this to the Corinthians. "The Lord Jesus, on the night he was betrayed, took bread, and when he had given thanks, he broke it and said, 'This is my body, which is for you; do this in remembrance of me'" (1 Corinthians 11:23–24).

Sunday

For centuries the Jews had kept Saturday as a special day in keeping with the rest of God in completing the work of Creation. But gradually Sunday began to replace Saturday as the weekly day of celebration. And why? Because of the Resurrection!

Having gone through all of this, we can see why it is that the Resurrection may be regarded as the most probable and plausible explanation of the historical evidence. And just when we think we are about to put a lid on the discussion and move on to the next chapter, someone from the back of the room suggests politely, "There are all kinds of stories in pagan literature of dying and rising gods. Do you not think it possible that the writers of the New Testament were simply creating a Christian version of these 'resurrection myths'?" At this point I am most grateful for the insight of Alister McGrath when he points out that "there are no known instances of this myth being applied to any *specific historical figure* in pagan literature." In other words, the ahistorical approach of mythology is in striking contrast to the focus on person, place, and date in the resurrection of Jesus. I am equally glad of McGrath's recollection of the wisdom of C. S. Lewis, and particularly, "Lewis's realization that the Gnostic redeemer myths—which the New Testament writers allegedly took over and applied to Jesus—were to be dated from later than the New Testament itself. If anyone borrowed from anyone, it seems it was the Gnostics who took up Christian ideas."[10]

One final comment. It is quite commonly suggested that there is no reason to spend time arguing for the historicity of the Resurrection because, it is alleged, the resurrection was a *symbolic* event which the first Christians took to be historical because they did not know any better. The idea behind this is the view that it was easy for the first Christians to believe in the resurrection of Jesus because belief in resurrections was commonplace. In fact, this was not the case. While there was a general anticipation of some form of resurrection on the last day, it is safe to say that no one expected what happened! The Sadducees denied any idea of resurrection. So the pump was not, as critics wish to suggest, primed in favor and prospect of the resurrection of Jesus at a certain place and in a moment in time. To dismiss the Resurrection as a historical event because it conformed to popular belief is to miss the point altogether. Although we may have become used to the notion, at the time it occurred it was

"wildly unorthodox and radical," and, for that reason as much as any other, it called for careful investigation.

So what do you think? In reviewing the evidence,
do you think it was the disciples' faith which engen-
dered the fact, or is it not more likely that the
reverse is true? *It is not by believing that we make it
happen. Rather it is because it has happened that we
have a basis for belief.* When Paul broached the subject in Athens, there was an immediate threefold
reaction on the part of his listeners. Some sneered,
some believed, and doubtless the largest group
delayed a decision, pending further considerations.
Assuming that you find yourself with the majority
at this point, can I encourage you to stay with me?

5

More Than a Man

Dr. Benjamin Jowett, the master, scholar, and wit of Balliol College, Oxford, was once asked, "Dr. Jowett, we would like to know your opinion of God." "Madam, I should think it a great impertinence were I to express my opinion about God. The only constant anxiety of my life is to know what is God's opinion of me." As the men of Athens listened to Paul, they were brought to the realization that their lives were moving inexorably to an appointment they could not avoid. And so are we. God has written into the divine calendar *"a day when he will judge the world with justice by the man he has appointed. He has given proof of this to all men by raising him from the dead"* (Acts 17:31, italics added).

By now we should be agreed, that if Jesus is not alive, the bottom falls out of Christianity. It is for this reason that I suggested Paul started here when he was talking with the people in Athens. He wanted his listeners to understand that the Resurrection provided the unmistakable proof that the story he was telling about Jesus as Judge and Savior was true. When we read the Gospels, we discover that it took the Resurrection for the light to turn on in the disciples' minds. It was only when they saw Him alive that they began to really understand the significance of His claims and the real nature of His mission. The honesty of the gospel writers is striking. Luke records how the disciples told "the stranger" on the road to Emmaus that they had hoped (note the past tense) that Jesus was the Redeemer of Israel (Luke 24:18–21). When their eyes were opened and they recognized Him, they dashed the seven miles back to Jerusalem to tell the others (vv. 33–34). It was while they were deep in conversation that Jesus appeared to the group; and far from being predisposed to believe Him alive, Luke admits that they thought they saw a ghost! Jesus proceeds to go through a process of convincing them. First He told them to *look* and then to *touch*, and finally He ate a piece of fish in their presence as much as to say, "See, ghosts don't eat!"

> He said to them, "This is what I told you while I was still with you: Everything must be fulfilled that is written about me in the Law of Moses, the Prophets and the Psalms."
> Then he opened their minds so they could understand the Scriptures. He told them, "This is what is written: The Christ will suffer and rise from the dead on the third day, and repentance and forgiveness of sins will be preached in his name to all nations, beginning at Jerusalem." (Luke 24:44–47)

Pretty soon the early Christians were singing hymns that summarized this mystery:

He appeared in a body,
　　was vindicated by the Spirit,
was seen by angels,
　　was preached among the nations,
was believed on in the world,
　　was taken up in glory.

(1 Timothy 3:16)

Now there are clearly some *difficult parts* in this statement. Here we find ourselves face-to-face with the facts that form the basis of some of the lines from our Christmas carols over which we stumble on an annual basis. Phrases like "very God of very God," "begotten, not created," "our God contracted to a span, incomprehensibly made man," "veiled in flesh the Godhead see, hail the incarnate deity." The New Testament writers could never be accused of simply trotting out some sloppy sentimentalism. The notion of making the Christian faith easy to believe obviously never occurred to them! When I encounter those who dismiss Christianity as "nothing more than a bunch of infantile stories generated by the clueless to offer to the unsuspecting," I wonder if they have ever seriously read the Bible and considered the staggering statements it contains. The idea of a small group getting together to "start" a religion and "coming up with" the idea of a triune God who is one in three and three in one, co-equal and coeternal—arguably the most difficult thought that the human mind has been asked to handle—is beyond my comprehension. Surely they would have "invented" a religion that was much more accessible. But instead, we have miracles, the Resurrection, a supernatural departure from the world by ascension—and let us not forget that

Christ's mode of entry into incarnate life was, as we would expect, equally supernatural, Mary having become pregnant by the Holy Spirit's creative action without any sexual relationship! (Matthew 1:20; Luke 1:35).

Rather than considering these Christian essentials as barriers to belief, let them serve as the building blocks for the kind of resolute faith that takes God at His word. You ought not to think that a Christianity with the difficult parts removed would be more acceptable on account of being more accessible. Those who have attempted to offer a trimmed down version of the Christian faith—by dispensing with the miracles and denying the Virgin Birth and offering a resurrection that is spiritual but not physical or historical—have discovered that sensible people have concluded that "there is nothing in it," and of course they are right. A moment's thought should serve to convince you that, for example, turning the divinity of Jesus into an optional extra is not like removing an appendix but rather the heart. "Only a form of Christianity which is convinced that it has something distinctive, true, exciting and relevant to communicate to the world in order to transform it will survive."[1]

This is the Christianity which Matthew, Mark, Luke, and John record for us. Let me encourage you to read these gospels carefully. We should bear in mind that the gospel writers were not ultimately biographers or even historians; they were evangelists. John informs us that his purpose in writing was to secure converts. "But these are written that you may believe that Jesus is the Christ, the Son of God, and that by believing you may have life in his name" (John 20:31). He has not written an impartial history, but rather has recorded the events of the life and ministry of Jesus in such a way as to fulfill his stated purpose. His gospel does not contain an exhaustive record of every miraculous sign and event; but the historical material John provides confronts each reader with the identity of Jesus, the necessity of faith, and the reality of eternal life.

JESUS IS GOD

As we consider some of the claims that Jesus made, we recognize that these claims do not in themselves constitute evidence. After all, each of us has probably met individuals who, often for the saddest of reasons, made some pretty bizarre claims about their identity. However, in the case of Jesus, we are confronted by material that demands an explanation.

Last year a young female singer rocketed to fame by combining a contemporary melody with an old question, "What if God was one of us?" In answer to this, John says, "He was!" Introducing his gospel, he describes what happened in the nativity scene in Bethlehem. "The Word became flesh and lived for a while among us. We have seen his glory, the glory of the One and Only Son, who came from the Father, full of grace and truth" (see John 1:14). By the use of words we communicate with one another. By describing Jesus as "the Word," John emphasizes that He is the One through whom God speaks fully and finally to us. Here, then, is the staggering claim. The baby cradled in the arms of Mary, at whom the shepherds gazed and before whom the wise men bowed, is none other than God!

So the birth of Jesus in Bethlehem in a stable was not the beginning of His existence.

Jesus' *human* life began at Bethlehem, but it was not the beginning of His existence. He enjoyed fellowship and glory with the Father before the world began. 'And now, Father, glorify me in your presence with the glory I had with you before the world began' (John 17:5). The One born in Bethlehem, who walked the hills and streets of Galilee, was the Creator of the universe, the mighty God. He preceded time, and He is above time.[2]

It therefore follows that it is on account of who He is that He does what He does. The religious leaders were jealous, and when they accused Him of "making himself equal with God," He did not back away. In fact He made the point with greater forcefulness. "Jesus gave them this answer: 'I tell you the truth, the Son can do nothing by himself; he can do only what he sees his Father doing, because whatever the Father does the Son also does. . . . For just as the Father raises the dead and gives them life, even so the Son gives life to whom he is pleased to give it'" (John 5:19, 21). Jesus knew that His challengers understood from the Old Testament that the giving of life is the prerogative of God alone. He therefore let it be known indirectly that the reason He was able to speak of Himself as One who gives life was because He is actually God.

This was to be established in the most dramatic fashion when He called for Lazarus, a dead man, to come out of the tomb in which he had been laid some four days previously. The religious authorities were frustrated by the impact Christ was making. They said more than they know when they declared, "If we let him go on like this, everyone will believe in him" (John 11:48). Their spite and jealous hatred extended to plans to kill Lazarus as well!

On another occasion, Jesus told his opponents that Moses wrote about Him and declared, "Before Abraham was born, I am!" (John 8:58). Now although this may not seem immediately striking, when we consider the reaction of the Jews we will begin to grasp the immensity of what Jesus was saying. John tells us that on the basis of these words from the lips of Jesus, "They picked up stones to stone him" (v. 59). This seems like overkill for the strange claim of being older than Abraham. That obviously was not their concern. Nor was even the suggestion of His eternity. Stoning was the punishment for blasphemy, and Jesus was using the phrase by which Jehovah had revealed Himself to Moses at the burning bush (Exodus 3:13–14). The reason His antagonists reached for the stones was that they heard Him take this divine title as a means of identifying Himself. They were in no doubt that He was claiming to be God.

If you take time to read John's gospel through, you will discover these amazing statements:

> If you knew me, you would know my Father also. (8:19)
> When a man believes in me, he does not believe in me only, but in the one who sent me. (12:44)
> When he looks at me, he sees the one who sent me. (12:45)
> If you really knew me, you would know my Father as well. (14:7)
> Anyone who has seen me has seen the Father. (14:9)
> He who hates me hates my Father as well. (15:23)

When we put all this together, we are led inescapably to the conclusion that to know Jesus was to know God, that hatred for Him was hatred of God, that to see and believe in Him was to see and believe in God. These categorical statements make clear that while we may choose to reject Jesus, we cannot set Him aside on account of His being something other than He claimed to be.

> Jesus was not just a God-inspired good man; nor was he a super-angel, first and finest of all creatures, called "god" by courtesy because he is far above men. Jesus was, and remains, God's only Son, as truly and fully God as his Father is. God's will, said Jesus, is that all may honor the Son, even as they honor the Father.[3]

But, you may be asking, What about others who have walked across the stage of human history and made some significant religious statements? What makes Jesus different from, say, Mohammed, who was born in 570 and at the age of forty emerged from a month's solitude in a mountain cave near Mecca to introduce his new religion of Islam? Well, for one thing, unlike Mohammed or any other religious leader, Jesus was expected! Hundreds of years before His coming, Isaiah described the scene that would unfold. "The people walking in darkness have seen a great light; on those living in the land of the shadow of death a light has dawned" (Isaiah 9:2). Micah prophesied the arrival of Christ in Bethlehem some six hundred years before it happened!

> But you, Bethlehem Ephrathah,
> Though you are little among the thousands of Judah,
> Yet out of you shall come forth to Me
> The One to be ruler in Israel,
> Whose goings forth have been from of old,
> From everlasting.
>
> (Micah 5:2 NKJV)

Isaiah prophesied about the servant of the Lord who will bring justice to the nations and will deal in gentleness and kindness with the bruised reeds and smoldering wicks (Isaiah 42:1–4). In the Synoptic Gospels we have the record of the healing of the man with a shriveled hand (Matthew 12:9–13; Mark 3:1–6; Luke 6:6–11). As a result, the Pharisees plotted how they might kill Jesus, and He withdrew and He healed those who followed Him. Matthew tells us (vv. 15–21) that this was to fulfill what was spoken through the prophet Isaiah in Isaiah 42:1–4, the section to which we have just referred. There are literally hundreds of these prophecies in the Bible, and they lend affirmation, not only to the deity of Christ, but also to the authority of Scripture.

JESUS IS THE LIGHT OF THE WORLD

"I am the light of the world. Whoever follows me will never walk in darkness, but will have the light of life" (John 8:12).

The people of Jesus' day were familiar with the significance of such a statement. The Pharisees declared that the name of the Messiah was Light, and the word *light* was especially associated in Jewish thought and language with God. After some four hundred years of prophetic silence, God commissioned "the Baptist John" to announce the arrival of Christ. His identity and role were clear. "He came as a witness to testify concerning that light, so that through him all men might believe. He himself was not the light; he came only as a witness to the light. The true light that gives light to every man was coming into the world" (John 1:7–9; see also the NASB reading).

The apostle John was declaring that only *in* Jesus and *through* Jesus is it possible to discover the light which is able to dispel the darkness. There may be ways to manufacture a few momentary flickers in the corners of our lives, but the permanent transformation of our darkness is only found in Him who is the Light of the World.

The majority of Jesus' listeners would have been involved in some way with the ceremony called "the illumination of the temple," which took place during one of the feasts. It took place in the court of the women, which was surrounded with deep galleries erected to hold spectators. In the center, four great candelabra were prepared, and when darkness came, they were lit. The effect in the city was dramatic. In a moment, the light changed everything, but of course it only lasted for a while. Jesus was able to teach by contrasting the light from the candles with the light that He was able to bring. First, your light only lasts for one exciting evening. But in Me there is not only the light *of* life but there is light *for* life. Second, the temple light is bright, but it flickers and dies. I am the light that lasts forever. Third, the source of your light is earthly. The source of My light is heavenly. Jesus says, "I am the light which is in itself life." The point is very clear: If men and women are to know real life, then they must come to *the* Light.

This claim brings us face-to-face not only with the identity of Jesus, but it also confronts us with our predicament. One of the recurring pictures the Bible uses to describe the human condition is darkness. "The way of the wicked is like deep darkness; they do not know what makes them stumble" (Proverbs 4:19). You would think that we would want to run for the light, but because our activities do not stand up to the scrutiny which the light brings, we actually prefer to live in darkness. Of course, we tell ourselves, "It's not *that* dark." Ours is not the darkness of those sordid dens of crime we find in Charles Dickens's novels. C. S. Lewis points out that the greatest evil isn't done in such places. "It is conceived and moved, seconded and carried and minuted, in clean, carpeted, warmed and well-lighted offices, by quiet men with white collars and cut fingernails, and smooth-shaven chins, who do not need to raise their voices."[4] This is not unique to our time. In the fourth century, Chrysostom said this about his culture: "Like men with sore eyes; they find the light painful, while the darkness which permits them to see nothing is restful and agreeable."

On the day that Adam and Eve refused to do the one thing God asked of them or, if you like, chose to do the one thing they had been asked not to do, the lights went out. They turned their backs and ran and hid. They were alienated and discovered guilt and shame. They became suspicious and blamed each other. Their family fell apart. Their boys' feud ended in death. This sad story is duplicated ad nauseam in this morning's newspapers. Meanwhile, in the coffee shops and bookstores the people come and go with talk of Michelangelo—and of extraterrestrials and out-of-body experiences and global warming, as if by such discussions they might turn the lights back on. Woody Allen cut through it when he said: "There will be no solution to the suffering of mankind until we reach some understanding of who we are, what the purpose of creation was, what happens after death. Until those questions are resolved, we are caught."

Trapped in the darkness, many lives are barely illuminated by the dim glow of the TV or computer screen, which invites them to escape into a world of virtual reality where images take the place of words, reason is replaced by emotion, and relationships are controlled with a password. The words of Jesus remain as timely in our cyberspace world as they were for the Jerusalem crowds. "I have come into the world as a light, so that no one who believes in me should stay in darkness" (John 12:46). Every so often we hear a voice from the darkness crying for a light to walk by and a companion to walk with. "I don't even know what my soul is," said one Hollywood producer. "I can't make a connection to God. It's a hopeless feeling that I'm all on my own. It's been this way for twenty years. I'd just like to know for one day what it feels like to hand your life over to God and say: 'Whatever will be, I accept.'"

The point is very clear. If men and women are to know real life, they must come to the light. Into the darkness of their *lies*, Jesus comes as the *truth*. To the darkness of *ignorance*, He is their *wisdom*. The darkness of their *impurity* is to be flooded with the light of His *holiness*. The darkness of their *grief* and loss overtaken by the light of His *joy*. And the darkness of physical and spiritual *death* exchanged for the reality of eternal light and *life*.

6

A Matter of
Life and Death

A man who is merely a man and said the sort of things Jesus said would not be a great moral teacher. He would either be a lunatic—on a level with a man who says he is a poached egg—or else he would be the devil of hell. You must make your choice. Either this man was and is the Son of God: or else a madman or something worse. You can shut him up for a fool; you can spit at him and kill him for a demon; or you can fall at his feet and call him Lord and God. But let us not come with any patronizing nonsense about his being a great human teacher. He has not left that option open to us. He did not intend to."[1]

If we allow the ideas of the last chapter to sink in, we will perhaps begin to feel a little less comfortable with the idea that Jesus was just another religious figure on the stage of human history. It becomes clear that the claims He made do not allow for such a conclusion. In thinking along these lines, the opening quote from C. S. Lewis has never been bettered.

Jesus was either a bad man or a madman or the God-man. The standard explanation of His being just a good religious teacher does not fit the facts. Jesus is dramatically different from other religious teachers. By His claims and His character He did not merely point toward God, He declared Himself to *be* God. If we go no further than the eighth chapter of John's gospel, we have more than enough material to reinforce the point. If you have access to a Bible, you may want to turn to this chapter and check this out with me.

THE LIGHT OF THE WORLD

As we have just seen, Jesus declared Himself to be the Light of the World. "I am the light of the world. Whoever follows me will never walk in darkness, but will have the light of life" (John 8:12). Contained in this was the implicit invitation to follow Him and to discover what it means to leave darkness behind and to live life in the light. There are numerous illustrations of this principle at work in the lives of individuals whom Jesus met along the way.

One of these is recorded by Luke, who tells the story of the encounter between Jesus and a wealthy tax collector from Jericho. It would appear from the story (Luke 19:1–10) that Zacchaeus was well known for being small and for being sinful, the latter on account of the notorious relationship between tax collecting and cheating. Tax collectors were known for lining their pockets by extorting money beyond the tax or levy they were entitled to collect. It would seem that the way the system worked made it virtually impossible to be a part of it without sharing in the "dark side of it all."

Being a small man, Zacchaeus had climbed a tree in the hope that he would get the chance to see what Jesus looked like. His interest in Christ may have been somewhat similar to yours. You are reading this book because you want to find out what sort of person Jesus was. Zacchaeus never bargained for the fact that he had unwittingly given himself a ringside perch! Jesus stopped under the tree and then He looked up into the tree and then He invited Zacchaeus to come down from the tree. "Zacchaeus, hurry up and come down. I must be your guest today" (Luke 19:5 PHILLIPS).

Can you imagine! Only a short time before, as he secured his vantage point, he had been hoping for a glimpse—and now here he is welcoming Jesus gladly as his guest.

When the crowd that had gathered saw this encounter taking place they began to mutter about how Jesus had gone to be the guest of a sinner. They found that totally incongruous. We might have predicted that reaction but not the response of the little tax collector. He came clean! He stepped into the light and immediately gave away half of his possessions and promised that if he had cheated anybody out of anything he would pay back four times the amount. Jesus explained the theology of what had happened: "Today salvation has come to this house. . . . For the Son of Man came to seek and to save what was lost" (Luke 19:9–10).

We do not have any details about this man's family or social circle, and we add nothing to the story by speculating. What we can safely infer is that his possessions did not satisfy him. If he had been totally convinced of the rightness of his actions and perfectly happy with his circumstances, then he probably would not have been up the tree in the first place and certainly not making the pronouncement that he did. In this respect he is like so many of us. I remember sitting having breakfast with a well-respected, highly successful trial lawyer. He told me that he had attended a breakfast where a Christian physician had spoken about an individual who had climbed the ladder of success to the top rung. It was only then that he recognized that his ladder was, as he put it, propped against the wrong wall. My friend told me how he had seen himself in that picture, and his conversion from darkness to light had come by way of a ladder, not a tree. This picture is too familiar for us to miss or deny. Ecclesiastes, one of the Old Testament books, contains this sad scene:

> There was a man all alone;
>> he had neither son nor brother.
> There was no end to his toil,
>> yet his eyes were not content with his wealth.
> "For whom am I toiling," he asked,
>> "and why am I depriving myself of enjoyment?"
> This too is meaningless—
>> a miserable business!
>
> (Ecclesiastes 4:8)

Over the past twenty-two years I have met many busy, popular, successful individuals who fit this description. They have an investment portfolio that is well diversified, carefully planned, and apparently secure. But they have made no provision for the matter of their soul. Michael Green tells how Annigoni wanted to be remembered by one of the twelve canvases he had painted on the subject of solitude because, he said, "The whole conviction of my life rests upon the belief that loneliness, far from being a rare and curious phenomenon peculiar to myself and a few solitary men, is the central and inevitable fact of human existence."[2]

There is a sense in which this is true. Sin alienates us from God, who made us, and then from one another, and also, strikingly, from ourselves. Generation X favors dark clothes, listens to dark lyrics, and is honest enough to admit to having dark, disturbing doubts about religion, meaning, purpose, hope, the future, even friendship. Maybe it's because I'm past the halfway mark or that I have forgotten what the sixties were really like, but as I sit in the mall and watch young people gather, there appears to be among them an almost palpable sense of futility. How often do we hear the culprit in a senseless shooting spree described as having been a loner. While the Beatles wondered about "all the lonely people," Paul Simon summarized the predicament in his song about a "most peculiar man" who had no friends and seldom spoke. As a result, no one in turn ever spoke to him because he wasn't friendly and he didn't care.

I recently read the obituary of Bob Merrill, the composer and lyricist. He was responsible for the nation tapping its toes to the novelty hit "How Much Is That Doggie in the Window?" He also wrote the lyrics for the Broadway musical *Funny Girl*. He penned the lines about "people who need people" being "the luckiest people in the world." Despite his success and the Beverly Hills address it afforded him, he suffered from prolonged depression and was found dead in his car in Culver City,

California, having taken his own life with a pistol. The call of Jesus is from such darkness to the light.

The invitation to follow Christ is one that, as we shall see, we must respond to individually, but in doing so we are immediately brought into wonderful company. The New Testament describes it in terms of being adopted into God's family and consequently finding ourselves in the company of brothers and sisters who are equally the beneficiaries of the Father's initiative.

ONE WITH THE FATHER

Jesus told the Pharisees, "If you knew me, you would know my Father also" (John 8:19). Later on, in chapter 14, when Jesus reiterated this statement, Philip, one of the disciples, replied, "Lord, show us the Father and that will be enough for us" (v. 8). In responding to His disciple, Jesus provided this categorical statement which should leave us in no doubt whatsoever concerning His identity: "Don't you know me, Philip, even after I have been among you such a long time? Anyone who has seen me has seen the Father. How can you say, 'Show us the Father'?" (v. 9).

I recall hearing of a schoolboy who, along with his classmates, was fulfilling the teacher's assignment to paint a picture of something that was important to them. When the teacher inquired about his subject matter, the boy informed her that he was painting a picture of God. "But we don't know what God looks like," said the teacher. To which the precocious youngster retorted, "Come back in about twenty minutes and you'll find out!"

"So close was his identification with God that it was natural for Jesus to equate a man's attitude to

Himself with his attitude to God," says John Stott, summarizing this fact as follows:

> to know him was to know God;
> to see him was to see God;
> to believe in him was to believe in God;
> to receive him was to receive God;
> to hate him was to hate God;
> to honor him was to honor God.[3]

Now remember, as we saw in the story of Zacchaeus, Jesus' mission was a rescue mission. He came to earth "to seek and to save what was lost" (Luke 19:10). "For God so loved the world that He gave His only begotten Son, that whoever believes in Him should not perish but have everlasting life" (John 3:16 NKJV). So when, as the hymn from 1 Timothy 3:16 puts it, "He appeared in a body," Jesus became what He was not, namely, a man, without ever ceasing to be what He was, namely, God. "Christ did not become God, but He who was God became a Man by taking our nature into His. He was not somebody in between God and man, a demigod or superman, but He was both God and man."[4] This truth is a cornerstone of basic Christianity. The deity of Jesus Christ is the essential presupposition of the finality of Christian revelation and the validity of Christian redemption. If Jesus is not Immanuel, God with us, then His revelation is not final and may be superseded. If we deny Christ's deity, then we are destined to grope forever in the darkness of our unenlightened reason. If Jesus is not who He claimed to be, then His death for our sins is of no value and does not in any way alter our standing before God. Consequently, any sense that we may have of peace and forgiveness would be just feelings and nothing more. He may have been a superstar, but a mere man could never be our Savior.

HIS IDENTITY
A MATTER OF LIFE AND DEATH

Jesus pointed out that the question of His identity was a matter of life and death. This is something we must keep in mind as we consider this material. "Unless you believe that I am who I am, you will die in your sins" (John 8:24 PHILLIPS). If any of us have been cherishing the illusion that we are, in this journey, pursuing matters of speculative interest, considering notions of being, or playing a kind of philosophical chess, this should serve as a rude awakening! God warned Adam and Eve that if they disobeyed His command they would surely die (Genesis 2:16–17). So it is that death became part of human existence. When you read the Old Testament account, your first thought may be, *But Adam and Eve did not die. They continued to live.* Not so. They were from that point *physically* alive and *spiritually* dead. The communion they had enjoyed with God in all the pristine beauty of that Paradise was broken, and the fact of alienation and the consequent need for reconciliation became a reality. So it is for us today. Men and women are aware of the undeniable fact of physical death. It is the great leveler —one out of one dies! It is referred to as the Grim Reaper. It is shrouded in mystery and uncertainty. When Shakespeare's Hamlet contemplates the inevitability of it, he reasons :

> To die: to sleep;
> No more; and by a sleep to say we end
> The heart-ache and the thousand natural shocks

That flesh is heir to, 'tis a consummation
Devoutly to be wish'd. To die, to sleep;
To sleep: perchance to dream: ay, there's the rub;
For in that sleep of death what dreams may come
When we have shuffled off this mortal coil,
Must give us pause. . . .
But that the dread of something after death,
The undiscover'd country from whose bourn
No traveller returns, puzzles the will
And makes us rather bear those ills we have
Than fly to others that we know not of?
(Hamlet 3.1.60–68, 78–82)

Reasoning similarly, contemporary men and women see physical death as the ultimate obstacle to be overcome. They approach it kicking and screaming or with grim resignation or with paralyzing fear. But at the funeral meal of loved ones all the talk is of how "They are at rest," as if somehow, by the saying of it, the mourner might make it so. Such an approach pays little attention to Jesus' reference to dying "in our sins." When we put together what the Bible has to say about death, we must face up to this. By nature, although we are physically alive, we are spiritually dead. Unless we in the course of our lives are made spiritually alive, then physical death plus spiritual death will lead to eternal death. There is a payday coming. When Paul declared it to the men of Athens, we are told that they began to argue about the Resurrection. Perhaps that was a defense mechanism to prevent them from having to face up to the dreadful thought of one day standing before the bar of God's judgment and facing His justice.

Jesus was perfectly and consistently clear about this issue. He spoke about the day when the people will be separated in the way a shepherd separates sheep from goats. Some people will go to eternal punishment and others will go to eternal life (Matthew 25:31–46). Jesus used such chilling language as speaking of unbelievers as being "cut . . . to pieces" and assigned "a place with the hypocrites, where there will be weeping and gnashing of teeth" (24:51). He urged his listeners to enter through the narrow gate, for "wide is the gate and broad is the road that leads to destruction, and many enter through it" (7:13).

Later in the New Testament, one of the writers puts the matter succinctly. "Man is destined to die once, and after that to face judgment" (Hebrews 9:27). Three times in the space of four verses Jesus uses the phrase "You will die in your sin[s]" (John 8:21, 24). Pay attention. Death has not yet reached out to us. Let it rattle its chains and stir us into action!

This is clearly of crucial significance and hinges on the truthfulness of the words of Jesus. He asks those who are challenging Him, "If I am telling the truth, why don't you believe me?" and, before that, "Can any of you prove me guilty of sin?" (John 8:46). And of course the answer is no. Neither the friends nor the enemies of Jesus could cast doubt upon the fact of His sinlessness. Peter referred in passing to Christ's perfection, speaking of Him as "a lamb without blemish or defect," One who "committed no sin, and no deceit was found in his mouth" (1 Peter 1:19; 2:22).

When Jesus was finally brought before the authorities, the charges were trumped up, and neither Herod nor Pilate was able to find fault in Him. As He hung upon the cross, one of the thieves pronounced His innocence. The penitent thief rebuked his friend for the way in which he was throwing insults at Jesus. What a wealth of insight is contained in his words: "Aren't you afraid of God even when you're getting the same punishment as he is? And it's fair enough for us, for we've only got what we deserve, but this man never did anything wrong" (Luke 23:40 PHILLIPS). Matthew tells us that when Judas threw the thirty silver coins into the temple, it was on account of his awareness that he had "betrayed *innocent* blood" (Matthew 27:4, italics added).

So whether we go behind the scenes with His disciples or listen to the accusations of His enemies or solicit the response of objective bystanders or take the testimony of the judges, we are forced to conclude that His character confirmed His claims. The compelling quality and worth and reliability of this Jesus is wonderfully appealing in an age when leadership tolerates a large gap between public pronouncement and private morality, when spin doctors help our leaders to speak out of both sides of their mouths while professing integrity, and while image is preferred above character. But that does not mean that all we are then saying is that Jesus was "far better" than anyone on the stage of human history at that moment. That is true, but the issue is far deeper. What we find is this: The goodness of Jesus is that of unparalleled moral perfection. It is nothing less than the goodness of God.

The crucial significance of this is found in the fact that here in Jesus we have One in whom there is no darkness at all! Our only hope of being led from the darkness is by One who Himself is unaffected by it.

The importance of this claim should be clear. Sin is a congenital disease. We are born with this infection in our nature. It is a universal complaint. Therefore if Jesus of Nazareth was without sin, He was not just man as we know men. If He was sinless, He was distinct from us. He was supernatural.[5]

If this were not the case, then Christ could not be our Savior. Only one who came from the outside could effect our rescue. Imagine that a group of us are hopelessly trapped under a huge steel beam which has immobilized us all. Intervention and liberation will have to come from the outside. It is pointless for us to expect that one who is himself trapped will also become the agent of rescue. Jesus stands alone on the stage of human history in this respect. I am unaware of any other religious leader who made a claim to sinlessness and certainly none, who if they chose to make such a claim, were able to substantiate it!

THE FREEDOM FACTOR

"Then you will know the truth, and the truth will set you free" (John 8:32). "So if the Son sets you free, you will be free indeed" (v. 36).

The fourth factor in pointing to the divinity of Jesus is what we can refer to as the "freedom factor." It follows from the last point that only one who is himself free can offer the possibility of freedom to those who are trapped. Perhaps the current level of interest in science fiction and the accompanying fascination with the idea of visitors from other planets is an indication that thinking people are certainly looking beyond themselves for a solution. The sexual revolution of the sixties can hardly be said to have ushered in the "free love" that it promised. The past three decades, instead of ushering in freedom, have introduced us to all kinds of bondage.

Perversion has replaced purity, self-love has replaced self-sacrifice, and instant sexual gratification has replaced long-term commitment. When Janice Joplin both lived and sang her cynical refrain, neither she nor her fans could have anticipated the tragic end to which her mantra would lead, not only her, but a whole succession of rock-'n'-rollers: "Freedom's just another word for nothin' left to lose. Freedom ain't worth nothin' but it's free . . ."

Having considered what happened to Zaccheus when he came face-to-face with "the truth," we now witness it at work in another life, a woman this time. You can find the actual account in John 4. I am allowing myself some poetic license by attempting to retell it in the first person.

I don't remember exactly when it was that I started going to the well in the middle of the day. I do know why I started—to avoid the angry glares and the sullen silences of the other women. I don't want to dredge through all the details. It's enough to say that when it comes to relationships with men, I have had a checkered history. Let's just say that the fact that I had had five husbands and then was living with a man I wasn't married to didn't endear me to the female population of Sychar!

I had the whole routine down to a fine art. I could walk to the well without really looking, and the picture never changed. Just the sun and the well and the water jar and me. That's why I was so startled when the stranger spoke. He'd obviously been sitting there watching me arrive, but I hadn't been paying attention, and so I was taken off guard by the encounter. First, because someone was there. Second, because the someone was a man. Third, because He was a

Jew, and fourth because He spoke to me. He asked me for a drink of water, and I recall commenting on how strange it was as a Samaritan woman to receive such a request from a Jewish man.

That, however, wasn't the strangest part. He said that if I had even half an idea about the gift of God and who it was who was asking, then I would have asked Him and He would give me living water. Living water! It makes you wonder who thinks these phrases up. Anyway, I thought I'd dealt the conversation a deathblow by observing that I couldn't see just how He was going to get this living water, and I also put Him in His place by asking whether He considered Himself greater than our father Jacob, who gave us the well and was quite happy to use it for himself and his family.

That didn't seem to faze Him at all. He said that drinking the well water would always leave you thirsty, but anyone who drank the water He gives would not only never thirst again but would discover his own eternal spring.

Count me in, I told Him, so that I could be done with these midday excursions.

Now to this point we had been talking without looking, but then He fixed me in His gaze, and of all the things for Him to say, 'specially when you realize that He knew nothing about me, He told me, "Go and call your husband and come back." I found myself instinctively looking down, and my voice hardly sounded like me when I replied, "I have no husband." You could have knocked me over with a feather when He went on to describe my circumstances. That's when I asked Him the question about worshiping. I think He made me feel guilty, and that in turn made me think about the need for sacrifice, and somehow that all came out as a comment about the where of worship. He turned immediately to the how, and I told Him that I was aware of the fact that when the Messiah (called Christ) comes, then it will all be worked out.

"I am Christ speaking to you now." That's what He said! And just as I was trying to figure it out, a whole bunch of His friends showed up. I can't recall whether I left the water jar because I thought they might need it or because I thought that I wouldn't. In any event, I left it behind and immediately went back to town, calling the people to come and meet this man. I'm sure at first they thought I must have lost it. I was walking through the market shouting, "Come see a man." "Another one," they must have been saying to themselves. "She's not satisfied with five husbands and a live-in lover—now there's another man!" But they came to Him, and then He stayed with us, and, you know, they said the most wonderful thing to me. "We no longer believe just because of what you said; now we have heard for ourselves, and we know that this man really is the Savior of the world." Isn't that wonderful!

It is clear that as a result of her encounter with Jesus, her life would never be the same again. Whatever deep-rooted sense of emptiness she had been trying to relieve by multiple relationships, she had clearly been unsuccessful. Sophia Loren spoke for more than herself when she said, "In my life there is an emptiness it is impossible to fill." Kirstie Alley just gave an interview to *USA Today* about her "lives, loves and passions." At the end of a journey that included reference to Scientology, drug and alcohol abuse, and her marriage in the 1400s to a man called Francesco (yes, that's right, the fifteenth-century!), she wrapped it up by saying, "I think you come to a point in your life . . . when you just decide that what's powerful is probably true love."[6]

The question remains: Where is this true love to be found? The answer we are finding is this: It is not discovered in a philosophy to be embraced, nor even in a creed to be followed, nor in a group to be joined, but in a *person*. It is in Jesus that we find ultimate freedom, love, life, forgiveness, family, and a future. The gospel writers tell us that when Jesus saw the crowds following Him, He saw them as sheep without a shepherd. But this is no ordinary shepherd. Jesus is the Good Shepherd who lays down His life for the sheep. When we come to the matter of the death of Christ, we are at the very nerve center of true Christianity.

THE PIVOTAL EVENT
OF HUMAN HISTORY

I read the obituaries most mornings in the *New York Times*. This is not due to a morbid fascination with death; just the opposite in fact. These well-written minibiographies provide one with a glimpse into the life and times of the subject. We discover where they were born and educated and a little about their family life. The emphasis is always upon whatever contribution they made to their little world and in turn to the wider culture. There is usually very little space devoted to the circumstances of their death. This is equally true in full-scale biographies. It is highly unusual to find more than a couple of paragraphs detailing the subject's death. Despite all the present focus on the death of Princess Diana, in years to come serious biographies will treat her demise with customary proportion. Their attention will be devoted to the significance of her life rather than the nature of her death.

In light of this, the thoughtful reader will be struck by the disproportionate space given to the death of Christ in the Gospels. More space is given to this than to any other event, including His birth, which, as we have seen, was marked by sights and sounds of unparalleled wonder. Now even allowing for the fact that the gospel writers were not historians or biographers but evangelists, this is still worthy of note. The explanation is straightforward. Christ's death was the main purpose of His coming. You might want to pause and think about that for a moment! The reason for His birth was His death. Throughout the centuries, some great minds have applied themselves to the immensity of this truth. In the twelfth century Anselm of Canterbury wrote a book that became required reading for every serious theological student. The question he sought to answer formed the title of his masterpiece, *Cur Deus Homo?* (literally, "Why God Man?"). In this treatise he quickly gets to the heart of the matter. The Atonement (we'll come to that word) is the real reason for the Incarnation. Or, if you like, Calvary is the real reason for Bethlehem. Or, as we might say to our children, the real reason for Christmas is Easter. J. I. Packer put it like this: "The crucial significance of the cradle at Bethlehem lies in its place in the sequence of steps down that led the Son of God to the cross of Calvary, and we do not understand it till we see it in this context."[7]

Anselm's answer runs along the following lines. First, our rescue had to be accomplished by God because He is the only One who could free us on account of the fact that He was not trapped. I am deliberately using our picture from the last chapter to make the point. We neither have the will nor the power to save ourselves, and so if we are to be saved then God must do it. Second, since man by his rebellion has placed himself into this mess, it should be a man who rights the wrong. It therefore follows that the rescuer must be both God and man, and that limits the candidates to one, namely, Jesus Christ. In attempting to reduce this profound mystery to a few simple sentences, we run the risk of making it all sound remote and algebraic. I have been helped by this statement:

> God Himself undertook to pay a cost, to offer a sacrifice, so tremendous that the gravity of his condemnation of sin should be absolutely beyond question even as he forgave it, while at the same time the love which impelled him to pay the price would be the wonder of angels, and would call forth the worshipping gratitude of the redeemed sinner.[8]

When the Magi finally arrived at the house, Matthew tells us, and saw the Child with His mother Mary, *"they bowed down and worshiped him"* (Matthew 2:11, italics added). However academic their search might have been, when they found themselves in His presence, their instinctive response was humble adoration. As we move around the scene of the Cross, we might think to slip off our shoes as we get the sense Moses had before the burning bush: We're treading on holy ground. I say this not to diminish our investigation but actually to enhance it. The psalmist reminds us, "You save the humble but bring low those whose eyes are haughty" (Psalm 18:27).

Let's suppose for a moment that we had arrived in Jerusalem on the day of the crucifixion of Jesus. Unfamiliar with the events of the preceding days, we would have been asking, "What in the world is going on here?" In one respect, the answer might have been, "Business as usual." After all, the execution of criminals was common practice, and the Romans were notorious for their use of this "most cruel and revolting punishment," as Cicero, a Roman writer, referred to it. Josephus, who recorded the crucifixion of two thousand rebels in 4 B.C., described crucifixion as "the most pitiable of deaths." Practiced first in Phoenicia and Carthage, it was taken up by the Romans; and although it was not a punishment permitted by Jewish law, those who lived in Judea under Roman occupation would have been only too familiar with the dreadful scene. It is surely worthy of note that none of the gospel writers provide any description of the physical details of the horrible process. They chose instead a simple statement of fact: "And they crucified Him." Is this perhaps because they knew that as dreadful and horrifying as the physical suffering of Christ inevitably was, His spiritual sufferings were greater? That, as Spurgeon put it, "The soul of His suffering was the suffering of His soul."

If we had inquired of someone who had been in the city during the previous twenty-four hours, we would have learned about the dramatic scene in the Garden of Gethsemane when one of Jesus' own band of disciples had betrayed Him with a kiss. Someone would have told us about the fact that only one of Christ's followers had made any attempt to resist the arrest of His master. He had swiped off one of the high priest's servant's ears and received an earful from Jesus for having done so! And when it came to the so-called trial, we would be forced to conclude that it was a travesty of justice. Let's think about it.

Consider the accusers of Christ. First of all, Annas. We might refer to him as "the godfather." He was the ruling power in Jerusalem. He is known in Jewish history because of the horrible way he rose to prominence. He and his sons accumulated vast wealth as a result of extortion and dreadful practices.

Then there was Caiaphas, also a nasty piece of work. If Annas was marked by shear blatant extortion, his son-in-law was craftier. He had absolutely no interest in justice. He was ready at any moment to elevate expedience over principle and pragmatism over truth. He was a cynical politician. He was a rude, sly, manipulative hypocrite. Matthew records how he tore his robes as an outward symbol of being overcome by profound sorrow when, in fact, he was inwardly delighted at the prospect of Christ's death. Christ was simply an obstacle to his popularity, and, like many after him, Caiaphas could not cope with that and wanted to be rid of Him.

And what of the official who struck Christ in the face? Even an ordinary man who was guilty would not have deserved such treatment. But for Jesus in His innocence and grace to receive such abuse is unthinkable. Who was this unnamed man? Did he expect to exploit the situation to his own advantage? Was he looking for a promotion? He's the kind of individual who likes to jump on the bandwagon, who runs to the front of the parade in order to "lead." He blows hot and cold depending upon what seems most suitable to achieve his despicable purposes.

Each of these accusers have their successors,

individuals who have heard the word of Christ have turned their backs to indulge their greed, then lust for popularity, and their craving for acceptance.

This was not a trial but a farce. There was no intention of giving Jesus the opportunity to declare His innocence of their trumped-up notions. Motivated by envy, they had already decided that Jesus must die. The religious leaders were losing ground, losing their hold on the people. Confronted as they were by their hypocrisy, they couldn't handle it. They were like many others, with a measure of decorum on the outside serving as a thin disguise for the vengeance, hatred, and death lurking in their cruel hearts.

This was not a trial but an orchestrated plot. The religious leaders devised it. They ordered officers to carry out the arrest. They found false witnesses. They delivered Christ to Pilate and stirred up the people to cheer for the release of the real criminal, Barabbas. They intimidated Pilate. They mocked Christ. And they walked brazenly toward Calvary, having decided against Christ without having first humbled themselves to listen to His words and genuinely consider His powerful claims.

But what of the attitude and actions of Christ? What a lesson in integrity! He had spoken openly during His three years of ministry in Palestine, He told them, and by checking they could verify His claims. Jesus also gave us an object lesson in meekness. We witness here the drama of His absolute power under absolute control. This was not simply quietness or human niceness, a gentle personality, if you like. It was certainly not a lack of conviction. It was this Jesus who had forcefully cleared the temple of the moneychangers. Here we see the dignity and majesty of Jesus as He was confronted by despicable individuals seeking to a make a mark on history by leaving a mark on Christ.

What an astounding contrast! The earthly high priest, with his puny power, exalted himself; while the Great High Priest, who has unlimited power, humbled Himself in the face of abuse and scorn and suffering. He did not respond in kind but committed His cause to a higher court and a just Judge. Peter summarized it in his first letter. "When he was insulted he offered no insult in return. When he suffered he made no threats of revenge. He simply committed his cause to the One who judges fairly" (1 Peter 2:23 PHILLIPS). As we read the Gospels, it is clear that Jesus died not as the helpless victim of evil forces, nor as a result of some inflexible decree, but because He freely submitted to the Father's plan. He had come to do the will of the Father. As John Stott has said, "What dominated Christ's mind was not the *living* but the *giving* of His life."

And so on Calvary the Roman soldiers fulfilled their function with the efficiency and objectivity that marks the seasoned gravedigger. When Hamlet is perturbed to find the gravedigger singing at his task, Horatio explains, "Custom hath made it in him a property of easiness." As the Romans went about their business with studied indifference, they failed to recognize that this scene was far different from any other crucifixion in which they had been involved. Here, in the everyday events of Roman jurisprudence, the pivotal event of human history was taking place. As men and women wandered through their empty way of life, God was intervening in the act of redemption.

A DARK DAY

Having noted what we might refer to as the "routine elements" surrounding the event, we must at the same time pay careful attention to the unique aspects. None is more striking than the darkness which came over the whole land from what the gospel writers describe as the sixth to the ninth hour. If we did not know how time was calculated in ancient Palestine, we might be forgiven for questioning the significance of its having become dark a little early. That was not the case. The writers were counting from 6:00 A.M. So J. B. Phillips paraphrases the verse helpfully: "At midday darkness spread over the whole countryside and lasted until three o'clock in the afternoon" (Mark 15:33 PHILLIPS).

There should be no surprise in this. What father, if he could, would not turn out the lights upon such a dreadful spectacle as that of his son stripped and scorned, beaten and bloodied before the gaze of the passersby? It was only some thirty-six months since John the Baptist had pointed to Christ as "the Lamb of God, who takes away the sin of the world!" (John 1:29). Now, in a moment in time, this Lamb without blemish or defect, who was chosen before the foundation of the world, was bearing sin in His own body on the tree. The One who stumbled under the weight of the cross and was nailed between two thieves, who cried out, "Father, forgive them for they know not what they do," is none other than God incarnate! The hymn writer comments aptly:

Well might the sun in darkness hide
And shut its glories in,

When God the mighty maker dies
For man the creature's sin.

The darkness is also appropriate when we think of Jesus' statement, "This is the verdict: Light has come into the world, but men loved darkness instead of light because their deeds were evil" (John 3:19).

As the Jerusalem crowds walked around in this noonday darkness, it was a fitting symbol of the darkness of the whole world when men and women reject light and truth. There is an ironic symmetry between Christ's death and birth in this respect. His birth was heralded by bright light at the midnight hour, and here His death is marked by deep darkness in the middle of the day!

Of all the people present in Jerusalem at this time, there was one for whom these events had special significance: Barabbas. He had been quite unwittingly caught up in the drama when Pilate, the Roman governor, tried to find a way to release Jesus from custody. The background is this: As a gesture of goodwill, a public relations exercise, if you like, it was customary during this special feast to release a prisoner whom the people requested. The choice came down to either Jesus, with whom Pilate could find no fault, or Barabbas, a notorious prisoner who had committed murder in an insurrection. Pilate offered the crowd the release of Jesus, but stirred up by the chief priests, they went instead for Barabbas. Now whether Barabbas ever went anywhere near the scene of the Crucifixion we do not know, but we can be sure that he understood that the cross which had been rightfully prepared for him was occupied by Jesus. He must have said to himself, "That cross ought to be mine. He's dying in my place."

This brings us to the very heart of the matter. We have already seen that Jesus was sinless; in the language of the Old Testament, He was "a lamb without spot or blemish." We, on the other hand, as we considered early on, are sinful. We are all spots and blemishes. We are sinners who deserve to be punished. We realize, too, that since God is righteous He must judge and punish sinners. So here we are trapped.

It is when this truth dawns that men and women often become interested in religion. They determine to "start over," to "clean up their act," to "make amends." The trouble with this, simply put, is that we can't get into God's "good books" by our "good deeds." In fact, these religious activities, rather than helping us, will in the end prove to be a hindrance. For as long as we retain any vestige of hope that we can escape God's rightful judgment upon sin by our own endeavors, we will continue to try—and always in vain. So first we have to face up to the bad news of our condition: that we are sinners with nothing to offer in our defense and without any means of atoning for our sins.

Throughout this book, we have been using the word *gospel*. It means simply Good News. And the Good News is this: that God has provided in the death of His Son a substitute for sinners. Christ's purpose was to take the sinner's place and bear the punishment the sinner deserved.

A criminal finds himself in prison, locked in his cell. A visiting friend calls out to him: "I have good news for you." With eager expectation the prisoner demands: "What is it? Out with it!" The answer comes, "Be good." Well, might that drive the prisoner mad? Yet precisely that is the only message which some who call themselves evangelists have for the sinner. It is not good news. It is not news at all. Good news for the sinner is that provision has been made for his release from sin and hell.[9]

Hundreds of years before the coming of Christ the prophet Isaiah described the way in which He would be the sinner's substitute.

> But he was pierced for our transgressions,
>   he was crushed for our iniquities;
> the punishment that brought us peace was upon him,
>   and by his wounds we are healed.
> We all, like sheep, have gone astray,
>   each of us has turned to his own way;
> and the Lord has laid on him the iniquity of us all.
>   (Isaiah 53:5–6)

In the New Testament, Paul summarizes this same truth as follows: "God made him who had no sin to be sin for us, so that in him we might become the righteousness of God" (2 Corinthians 5:21).

It is this which explains Christ's death upon the cross.

> He had no sin of His own for which to make amends, so there was no reason why He should have died on the cross, apart from the plan of rescue. . . . [The] cross was no impersonal, detached act of rescue; He gave Himself on the cross, having a special interest in the result of His sacrifice. He joyfully anticipated the salvation of a countless number of men and women through His sacrificial act.[10]

A LOUD CRY

"At the ninth hour [three o'clock] Jesus cried out in a loud voice [in Aramaic], '*Eloi, Eloi, lama sabachthani?*'

—which means, 'My God, my God, why have you forsaken me?'" (Mark 15:34; cf. Matthew 27:46).

The darkness which had swallowed the city at midday was a fitting symbol of the darkness of soul which Christ experienced in having the accumulated sins of human history laid on Him. Earlier we noted that sin alienates us from God. It therefore follows that in becoming sin for us Jesus experienced the horrible reality of being cut off from His Father. He had, until that point, always known unbroken communion with the Father, both prior to and during His incarnation. But now the God who is too pure to be able to look on iniquity turns His face away from His Son, and out of the soul-rending agony of that separation comes this cry from Christ.

We must keep in mind that this was taking place according to the Father's plan. Timothy Rice wrote a powerful lyric in the Gethsemane song in the play *Jesus Christ, Superstar;* but whether by design or by default, by describing Christ as somehow trapped in a scheme devised by the Father, a begrudging participant in a sorry event, he missed this point altogether, namely, that the Father and the Son and the Holy Spirit worked in complete harmony in effecting the rescue of sinners. It is not uncommon to hear this dismissed by a caricature which portrays a helpless son trying to placate an angry father. Nothing could be further from the truth. The Bible teaches that it was the love of God the Father which drew up this rescue plan, the love of God the Son which accomplished it, and the love of the Holy Spirit which applies it to the heart of every penitent sinner. Again, Derek Prime:

The glorious truth is that God the Father took the complete initiative in all this and, because of His love for sinners, worked out and put into operation this amazing plan for us to be brought back to Himself. God Himself wishes to have men as spiritual sons so that they may call Him "Father." The plan is God the Father's—and so is the praise.[11]

It is only when we consider the Cross in light of the fact of sin and redemption that we can begin to understand why it is a demonstration of divine love. If we dwell simply on the event itself, we might reach all kinds of conclusions.

We might possibly learn that the One who died there was the Son of God, but even that fact as such provokes only wonder and puzzlement; we could note that the form of death was such as to involve copious blood-shedding, but again no amount of mere pondering will bring us to any significant truth. Some insightful person might even say, "What a declaration of the love of God this is!" but this should only provoke the question "Why"—for what is there about dying as such to link it with love? On the face of it, it could be as much an act of folly as of affection. No, before it will yield up its secrets the bare act, the historical core, needs an ideological context.[12]

Unless the death of Christ has some direct end to answer in the redemption of the race, I confess myself unable to attach any meaning to the statement that the Death of Christ was a revelation of His love. . . . If my brother made his way into a burning house to save my child . . . and were himself to perish . . . his heroic fate would be a wonderful proof of his affection for me and mine; but if there were no child in the house and if I were told that he entered it and perished with no other object than to show his love for me, the explanation would be absolutely unintelligible. The statement that Christ died for no other purpose than to reveal His love to mankind, is to me equally unintelligible.[13]

A TORN CURTAIN

Matthew, Mark, and Luke all have a comment on the curtain, and it is surely important. "The curtain of the temple was torn in two from top to bottom" (Mark 15:38). Now this will not mean very much to us without a brief Old Testament lesson. The people were aware of the way that sin separated them from a holy God: "Your eyes are too pure to look on evil; you cannot tolerate wrong" (Habakkuk 1:13). The design of both the tabernacle and the temple reinforced the fact of separation. There was an outer room, which was called the Holy Place; and then an inner, smaller room, which was called the Most Holy Place, or the Holy of Holies. The barrier between the two rooms was a thick curtain. There was regular priestly activity in the outer room. The Most Holy Place was entered only once a year. The high priest went alone, taking with him a sacrifice of shed blood to be offered for his own sins and those of the people.

The architecture, if you like, was reinforcing what the Bible teaches and what our experience confirms: that we are, on account of our sins, separated from God and that even the best of these sacrifices were unable to clear the conscience of the worshiper. Why is it, we ask ourselves, that God seems so far away and that our religious exercises do not appear to bring God any closer? It is because of our sin we are aliens and strangers.

Now, getting back to the torn curtain, you have probably begun to put the pieces together. When Christ died in the place of sinners, He opened up a new and living way to God. It was no longer going to be necessary or even possible for earthly priests to make sacrifices on behalf of the people because Christ, our great High Priest, had "offered for all time one sacrifice for sins" (Hebrews 10:12). And as a fantastic visual aid, God, as it were, reached in and tore the curtain so that the people would be in no doubt that the way into His presence was no longer restricted.

All of the sacrifices in the Old Testament pointed forward to the Cross, where Christ made a perfect sacrifice for sins. As we have seen, we are unable to atone for our sins. We cannot find a way to make amends, blot out our offenses, and put ourselves into a right relationship with God. If we could, there would be no need for God to present Jesus "as a sacrifice of atonement, through faith in his blood" (Romans 3:25). It is beyond the scope of this book to unpack the wonder of words like *redemption, reconciliation,* and *propitiation.* We have, I hope, understood why the hymn writer penned these words:

> *There was no other good enough*
> *To pay the price of sin.*
> *He only could unlock the gate of heaven*
> *And let us in.*

It is very humbling to recognize that for us to be put in a right relationship with God, we need to know only two vital truths. First, that we are great sinners; and second, that Christ is a great Savior. In other words, we plead in our defense what another has done on our behalf. Someone has put it this way:

> *Upon a life I did not live,*
> *Upon a death I did not die,*
> *Another's life, another's death,*
> *I stake my whole eternity.*

This goes against the grain of the individual who has grown up believing that with hard work and maybe a little "luck" you can achieve anything. However well that philosophy may appear to work in sports, academics, or business and social affairs, it certainly is useless when it comes to gaining entry to heaven. But isn't it strange that in this matter of redemption, someone else gets to take the test for us? Aren't the innocent supposed to be acquitted and the guilty condemned? Is it not then an unjust action on God's part to acquit the guilty?

Well, this takes us back once again to what we noted earlier about Jesus becoming sin for us. When we understand this, then we can see that for God to justify the sinner on the basis of what Christ has done is in fact a just judgment. On the basis of Jesus Christ's death the Father reckons to believers His Son's righteousness, pronouncing them free from all guilt and declaring them just and righteous before Him. Again, we have it in a hymn.

> *Because the sinless Savior died,*
> *My sinful soul is counted free.*
> *For God the just is satisfied*
> *To look on Him and pardon me.*

This justification is not a *process;* it is a single deci-
sive *event.* Its basis is entirely in what Christ has done,
and we receive divine pardon and acceptance as we
give ourselves in faith to Jesus. Charles Haddon Spurgeon, who was known in London at the end of the
nineteenth century as "the prince of preachers," put
the matter before his congregation in these words:

> All that God can demand of a believing sinner, Christ
> has already paid, and there is no voice in earth or
> heaven that can accuse a soul that believes in Jesus
> after that. You were in debt, but a friend paid your
> debt; no writ can be served on you. It does not matter
> that you did not pay it; it is paid and you have the
> receipt. That is sufficient in any fair court. So all the
> penalty that was due to us has been borne by Christ.
> It is true I have not borne it; I have not been to hell
> and suffered the full wrath of God, but Christ has suf-
> fered that wrath for me, and I am as clear as if I had
> paid the debt to God and suffered His wrath. Here is a
> rock upon which to lay the foundation of eternal
> comfort! Let a man get to this truth: my Lord outside
> the city's gate bled for me as my surety, and on the
> cross discharged my debt. Why then, great God, I no
> longer fear your thunder. How can you condemn me
> now? You have exhausted the quiver of your wrath;
> every arrow has already been used against my Lord,
> and I am in Him clear and clean, absolved and deliv-
> ered, as if I had never sinned.[14]

The language is a little quaint but the message is
crystal clear. In justifying the sinner God passes the
last judgment that will ever be passed on our destiny and He will never go back on it.

7

The Ultimate Scandal

Can I bring something?" That question is regularly on our lips when we are looking forward to enjoying the hospitality of a friend's home. Somehow we feel a little better about being on the receiving end of their generosity if we know that we have made at least a small contribution to the proceedings. The reply is usually more than gracious: "No, thank you. I don't want you to bring anything other than yourself!"

When it comes to salvation, our tendency, as we have seen, is to want to bring something, to make a contribution. We want to be able to point to the way in which we have been successful in keeping some of the Ten Commandments or to draw attention to our religious affections or our acts of kindness. Yet instead of God's law proving to be a ladder up which we can climb to heaven, it simply makes us conscious of our sin. It may make us feel a little better to find people who are "worse than us," but when we come to find out that God does not grade on the curve, we realize that an F is an F, and there is no use trying to bolster our self-esteem with the thought that ours was a "high F"! If we think of the gap between a holy God and sinful man as being like the distance across Niagara Falls, what comfort is there in knowing that we can jump farther than some? There will be those who can pass us up. The fact is, none can bridge the chasm by human ability. "There is no difference, for all have sinned and fall short of the glory of God, and are justified freely by his grace through the redemption that came by Christ Jesus" (Romans 3:22–23).

So, staying with our analogy, when someone asks the justified sinner how he came to be on the "other side," he can only point to what Christ has accomplished. He alone is the bridge over troubled waters. Or, to use our earlier picture, when the sheep that had become hopelessly lost and trapped on a cliff edge with no way of escape is gathered up in the arms of the seeking shepherd and brought into the warmth and safety of the fold, the praise must all be for the shepherd.

In light of the fact that no one can justify himself before God and that God justifies every man who has faith in Jesus Christ, the apostle Paul then asks the key question, "What happens now to human pride of achievement? There is no more room for it. . . . [The] whole matter is now on a different plane— believing instead of achieving" (Romans 3:27 PHILLIPS). This doctrine of justification by grace alone through faith alone was the storm center of the Reformation and understandably so, for it is the very core of the Good News (Romans 1:16–17). Instead of asking, "Can I bring anything?" the individual who has been grasped by this "amazing grace" declares, "Nothing in my hand I bring, Simply to Thy cross I cling . . .

> *Not the labors of my hands*
> *Can fulfill Thy law's demands;*
> *Could my zeal no respite know,*
> *Could my tears forever flow,*
> *All for sin could not atone;*
> *Thou must save and Thou alone.*

This is an unpopular message because it strips us of our pride. Our connections and accomplishments, which give us access to clubs and societies, count for nothing at this gatehouse. This is what Professor Nathaniel Micklem of Mansfield College, Oxford, referred to: "The ultimate scandal of evangelical religion . . . lies not in dogma or symbolism but in its intolerable offense to human pride."[1]

This is certainly confirmed in the conversations I have with the well-heeled businesspeople in the city of Cleveland. While they are willing, even keen, to consider the teaching of the Bible, they are distinctly uncomfortable with having to admit their spiritual bankruptcy. They have become so used to being "special" and of enjoying the privileges of the Red Carpet Club that they cannot comprehend that, on the flight to heaven, prostitutes and other *really* sinful types are already comfortably on the plane while they sit smoldering in the departure lounge. They refuse to board if they cannot board on their own terms. Now this is not unique to the successful, but Jesus did make no bones about the fact that it would be easier for a camel to go through the eye of a needle than for a rich man to enter the kingdom of heaven. Why? Because there is the great tendency to rely upon what we have and to use it as currency. However, while money may be regarded as the universal passport, it cannot secure entry to heaven.

Spurgeon also addressed his congregation on this issue. In the following quote he is describing those who dislike the plan of salvation because it crushes their pride.

> They would be comforted, but may they not do something to earn eternal life? May they not at least contribute a feeling or emotion? May they not prepare themselves for Christ? Must salvation be all gratis? Must they be received into the house of mercy as paupers? Must they come with no other cry but, "God be merciful to me a sinner?" Must it come to this—to be stripped, to have every rag of one's own righteousness torn away, even the righteousness of feeling as well as the righteousness of doing? Must the whole head be confessedly sick, and the whole heart faint, and the man lie before Jesus as utterly undone and ruined, to take everything from the hand of the crucified Savior? Ah then, says flesh and blood, I will not have it. The banner of self is held up by a giant standard bearer; it floats on long after the battle has been lost. But what folly! For the sake of indulging a foolish dignity we will not be comforted. Down with you and your dignity! I beseech you, bow down now before the cross.[2]

There is no more obvious place to turn to consider this "scandal" than the parable told by Jesus about the Pharisee and the tax collector. He gave this illustration to certain people who were confident of their own goodness and looked down on others.

Two men went up to the Temple to pray, one was a Pharisee, the other was a tax-collector. The Pharisee stood and prayed like this with himself, "O God, I do thank thee that I am not like the rest of mankind, greedy, dishonest, impure, or even like that tax-collector over there. I fast twice every week; I give away a tenth-part of all my income." But the tax-collector stood in a distant corner, scarcely daring to look up to Heaven, and with a gesture of despair, said, "God, have mercy on a sinner like me." I assure you that he was the man who went home justified in God's sight, rather than the other one. For everyone who sets himself up as somebody will become a nobody, and the man who makes himself a nobody will become somebody. (Luke 18:9–14 Phillips)

Here are two men who arrive at the same place, the temple, to engage in the same activity, prayer. One of them had significant social standing on account of his religious position. The other was at the opposite end of the spectrum altogether. The tax collector, as a breed, was despised on largely two counts: political collaboration and moral corruption. Jesus' listeners, who were becoming used to the "sting in the tale" that marked many of His stories, could hardly have been prepared for the conclusion of this one! The term Jesus used, *justified*, would have been understood by his hearers to have come from the law courts. The magistrates were charged with the responsibility of pronouncing verdicts. For the guilty they pronounced *condemnation*, and the innocent were declared *justified*. Solomon's words would not have been unfamiliar: "Acquitting the guilty and condemning the innocent—the Lord detests them both" (Proverbs 17:15).

That's the sting in the tail to which we are referring. On first blush it appears that Jesus is violating the Old Testament principle. This becomes apparent when we consider these individuals in more detail. The Pharisee was one of a relatively small group of separatists. These individuals worked hard at isolating themselves from "contamination." They stayed away from ceremonial impurity, the heathen, tax collectors, sinners, and even the rank and file of Judaism, whom they disregarded as ignorant of the Law. The Pharisees were consumed with externals. They had become expert at cultivating a hollow formalism that was ostentatious and self-serving. Jesus actually warned His disciples about such individuals in this stinging condemnation:

> Beware of the teachers of the law. They like to walk around in flowing robes and love to be greeted in the marketplaces and have the most important seats in the synagogues and the places of honor at banquets. They devour widows' houses and for a show make lengthy prayers. Such men will be punished most severely. (Luke 20:46–47)

The tax collector was a very different kettle of fish. Roman knights and wealthy men often used their assets to pay the Roman government a fixed sum of money for the rights to levy tolls and taxes in a specific area. These wealthy men were called "publicani" because they paid their purchase price into the public treasury (*in publicum*). They employed tax collectors to do the actual collections of tax from the people. It was customary for these tax collectors to charge whatever they could get away with. They knew what they needed to pass on to their superiors, and anything beyond that sum which they were able to secure was money in their pockets. So they were regarded as extortionists, and as Jews they were regarded as traitors to Israel because of the help they were giving to their foreign oppressors.

In terms of their status in society, to say it was low is an understatement! They were viewed as being at the very bottom of the pile, along with harlots and other disreputable types. To have a tax collector in your family was regarded as a public disgrace. The synagogue and temple did not receive their alms. Promises did not have to be kept to murderers, thieves, or tax collectors. Because they were held in such contempt, these individuals tended to become hardened against all better feelings and they defied public opinion. In light of this, perhaps Zacchaeus climbed the tree not only to be able to see but also to be safe!

The people who were listening to Jesus tell this story would have been in no doubt that these men represented two extremes: the pinnacle of self-righteousness and the depth of depravity. Their opinion of themselves becomes apparent as we listen to them pray. Both men regarded themselves as being in a class of their own. The Pharisee's prayer was loaded with self-congratulation. Listen to his use of the personal pronoun "I." He was praying about, or to, himself. He let it be known to whomever may have been listening that he was thankful that he was not like other men. After all, he avoided sin. He was clean when it came to theft, evil, adultery, and certainly the corrupt practices of the tax collectors. On the positive side, he practiced piety. When it came to praying, fasting, and giving, he was not simply fulfilling the minimum requirements. So we find him trusting in himself and looking down on others. His whole attitude was typical of the worst in Pharisaism.

"I thank you, Lord my God, that you have put my place in the Academy and not with those who sit at street corners. For I rise early and they rise early; I rise early to the words of the law, and they to vain things. I labor and they labor; I labor and receive a reward, and they labor and receive no reward. I run and they run; I run to the life of the world to come, and they to the pit of destruction." Rabbi Simeon ben Jocai once said, "If there are only two righteous men in the world, I and my son are these two; if there is only one, I am he!"

The tax collector also was thinking about himself. But he did not compare himself with others. His posture was penitent. With eyes downcast, he beat his breast and, recognizing what he deserved, cried to God for mercy. "God, have mercy on me, a sinner." "The tax collector was a rotter and he knew it. He asked God for mercy because mercy was the only thing he dared to ask for."[3]

How the listeners' jaws must have dropped when Jesus let it be known that it was the tax collector who went home from the prayer meeting justified. The Pharisee's problem was not that what he said was inaccurate; it was factual. His condemnation lay not in the fact that he was righteous, but because he was self-righteous. He was relying upon himself and his merits. The tax collector recognized that he had no merits and so could only cast himself on the promise of God's mercy. He was not justified simply because he was a sinner, but because he knew that to be the case and was appealing for mercy alone.

Perhaps a simple analogy will help drive the

point home. From time to time, I have to have a photograph taken for inclusion in a brochure for a conference at which I have been asked to speak. Over the years as a family we have had some great laughs reviewing the photographer's proofs. My wife and children have left me in no doubt that I have a wonderful face for radio! I learned very quickly that I should never tell the photographer that I wanted the "mug shot" to do me justice because I was sure he would quickly reply, "Alistair, what you require is not justice, but mercy!"

The Pharisee was confident that he was "in good shape" and so appealed for justice. The tax collector knew himself to be "in poor shape" and so looked humbly to God for mercy. This parable reinforces the truth that salvation is not something we earn but, rather, is a gift we receive. This is one of the clearest ways in which Christianity differs from the religious systems of the world. In each case they emphasize the necessity of tipping the scales in our favor by means of our good and meritorious deeds outweighing the bad. The ultimate scandal of Christianity is in this: that God is merciful to the undeserving, to sinners, to those who have no merit but the merit of Christ to plead, and no argument but the humble, believing cry, "God, be merciful to me a sinner!"

But this notion offends. A more contemporary explanation of the predicament of the tax collector would have been that he was suffering from a poor self-image and low self-esteem. In that case, he needed to think more positively about himself. He should take a leaf out of the Pharisee's book and bolster his position by reflecting on his good points. After all, it is said, there are plenty of "ways" to follow on the journey to heaven. Well, we would do well to listen to the words of Jesus: "I tell you the truth, I am the gate for the sheep. All who ever came before me were thieves and robbers, but the sheep did not listen to them. I am the gate; whoever enters through me will be saved" (John 10:7–9).

"But," says someone, "isn't this kind of assertion simply arrogant?" If it *isn't* true, it's not arrogant— it's irrelevant. If it *is* true, then it certainly isn't arrogant. The arrogance is to be found in the lives of those who refuse to humble themselves and make the tax collector's prayer their own. John Bunyan's *The Pilgrim's Progress* is full of fascinating characters. Early on, he introduces us to Formalist and Hypocrisy, who joined Christian on the "narrow way" by climbing over the wall. When Christian challenges them about the fact that they had not made entry by way of "the gate," they respond by pointing out that they had chosen instead to take a shortcut. They chided him for being so "particular," since people had been climbing over the wall for more than a thousand years. "Besides," said they, "if we get into the Way, what matter is it which way we get in? If we are in, we are in: thou who art but in the Way, who, as we perceive, came in at the gate; and we are also in the Way, that came tumbling over the wall; wherein now is thy condition better than ours?" Then we have Christian's striking reply: "I walk by the rule of my Master; you walk by the rude working of your fancies. You are counted thieves already by the Lord of the Way; therefore I doubt you will be found true members at the end of the Way. You came in by yourselves without His direction, and you shall go out by yourselves without His mercy."[4]

In the Old Testament we have a classic illustration

of this principle in the story of Naaman (2 Kings 5:1–14; cf. Luke 4:23–27). As commander of the army of the king of Aram, he had power and prominence. He enjoyed an enviable position and lived in a very desirable place. However, there was one factor that cast long shadows over all his proud achievements. He had leprosy. His physical condition is a picture of the spiritual condition each of us faces. All that the Bible tells us about sin is conveyed perfectly in this picture of leprosy. Naaman's predicament was ugly, and it obviously had no respect for his person. Neither his possessions, which were considerable, nor his power, which was significant, could grant him relief or afford him a cure. The rich and powerful are used to buying a solution, but in this case he was unable to do so. When the hint of a solution came, it was from an unexpected source. From the broom closet! A servant girl sends him to Elisha, who sends word to Naaman, directing him to go and dip himself in the Jordan seven times!

Now this is scandalous to the commander, who takes off in a rage. His response is classic: "I thought that he would surely come out to me and stand and call on the name of the Lord his God, wave his hand over the spot and cure me of my leprosy" (2 Kings 5:11). Like those we mentioned at the beginning of the chapter, he was interested in solving the problem provided the solution was in accord with his expectations. If he needed to dip in a river, he was familiar with far more "suitable" streams. He is insulted by the proposed solution. To his mind, it is both humiliating and ridiculous. The same is true of the Good News, which confronts us with our inability to contribute anything and calls for us to trust unreservedly in God's promise of cleansing and forgiveness. "If all we have to do is bow down and admit our need of God's mercy, then what is the value of my education and morality and my church attendance and my good works?" These things are not bad in themselves, but they contribute nothing to the cure we require. All that we bring is our poverty, hopelessness, and helplessness.

Naaman came very close to walking away from his only hope of cleansing. His servants urged him along these lines: "If the prophet had told you to do some great thing, would you not have done it? How much more, then, when he tells you, 'Wash and be cleansed'!" (v. 13). What was it that kept Naaman from following through on the prophet's directive? His pride. It was the ultimate scandal: that a powerful, prosperous, prominent individual such as he should have to humble himself in this way. Some who are reading this book may well toss it aside at this juncture. Others will realize that you must come and bow before the Cross of Christ and say with the hymn writer:

> *Just as I am, without one plea,*
> *But that Thy blood was shed for me,*
> *And that Thou bidd'st me come to Thee,*
> *O Lamb of God, I come! I come!*

8

Settling
the Accounts

There is no doubt that the majority of what we have considered in these chapters is in direct conflict with contemporary worldviews. Having seen that to be true of the Christian view about life's beginnings, it should be no surprise to find that the speculations of the late twentieth century regarding the end of life are at complete variance with what the Bible has to say. In my files I have a variety of newspaper and magazine articles on the question of death and what happens next. Headlines like "Faith: A Window to the Hereafter" are fairly common. What is most striking about the material is the abundance of speculation and the almost total absence of certainty. This inability or unwillingness to define terms and draw conclusions is in keeping with a culture that refuses to draw lines because it regards the drawing of lines as being rude. And so a variety of euphemisms—"passing on," "at rest," "gone to be with father"—are in many cases nothing more than a gentler way to describe the oblivion people expect. It is therefore no surprise that *death* is now society's only taboo topic.

> Despite what you were told, the last taboo in polite conversation is not religion or politics. And judging from what's on TV or in the headlines, and even in the funnies, the last conversational taboo certainly isn't sex. No, it's death.
>
> If you spend any time in hospitals, you don't need to be convinced of this fact. A family bravely soldiers on, refusing to discuss death with a dying relative. A doctor can't bring himself to tell a patient that the end is in sight, and finds refuge in euphemisms and false cheer.[1]

It is in this climate that Woody Allen's words express the cynical sentiments of many: "It's not that I'm afraid to die, it's just that I don't want to be there when it happens!"

"What was the final score?" We are familiar with that question from the world of sports. Recognizing that the game has been played according to rules, that penalties have been assessed and goals recorded, it is inevitable that when the final whistle blows there will be smiles for one team and tears for the other. Schoolyard soccer games were part of my daily routine as a schoolboy. On good days we had a large soccer ball, but we frequently did battle with just a tennis ball. There were no sidelines, and the goalposts were satchels or sweaters. Consequently, there were frequent debates as to whether the ball had gone between the sweaters and a goal had been scored, or if it had simply crossed the sleeve of the sweater and gone out of play for a goal kick or a corner. As difficult as those discussions proved to be, still the game went on. The one thing we never did was to attempt to play without rules and goals. To have done so would have made it impossible to assess the final outcome.

Although it is not uncommon to meet individuals who are convinced that they are playing the game of life without rules, they are in fact kidding themselves. They have at least one rule, namely, that there are no rules! Such individuals will argue vehemently for a heaven that will prove to be a "judgment free" environment. But they are hoping against hope. The Bible tells us that God "has also set eternity in the hearts of men," and with that comes an inevitable sense of judgment (Ecclesiastes 3:11). We live with an inbuilt awareness that the final score will be posted, that the test results will be made available, that despite the unfairness of life as we know it, God is going to balance the books and establish justice.

The reality of judgment is not something that we have to search hard for in the Bible. In the Old Testament, "the Preacher" ends his book by declaring, "God will bring every deed into judgment, including every hidden thing, whether good or evil" (Ecclesiastes 12:14).

The writer of Hebrews puts the matter succinctly. "Just as man is destined to die once, and after that to face judgment, so Christ was sacrificed once to take away the sins of many people" (Hebrews 9:27–28).

Paul writes to the Romans about the "day when God will judge men's secrets through Jesus Christ, as my gospel declares" (Romans 2:16).

The idea of a coming Day of Judgment is not unique to Christianity. Islam also teaches that there will be a final judgment. But there is a vast difference between the two when it comes to determining where an individual will spend eternity. For the Muslim, placement in eternal bliss or tribulation is going to be determined by how well the individual has done in ensuring that in this life the good has outweighed the bad. This concept is graphically depicted in the Islamic symbol of the scales. In contrast, in the verse above Paul relates the Day of Judgment to the person of Jesus. "This is an indication that the last judgment is essentially not a mere adding up of good deeds and bad deeds to see which outweighs the other. Instead it is a judgment which relates to our response to Jesus. Jesus was crucified for us, and died for us. What has been our response to that sacrifice?"[2]

Back with Paul in Athens we discover the same emphasis: "For he has set a day when he will judge the world with justice by the man he has appointed" (Acts 17:31). It is because the Bible is so clear concerning this issue that the Apostles' Creed, which is a helpful summary of true Christianity, refers to Christ coming from heaven "to judge the quick [the living] and the dead."

Despite this central emphasis, it is quite common to find this part of the truth missing from explanations of Christian faith. This, I assume, is largely due to a fear of appearing negative. We are so driven by the idea that in order to appeal to the mind of contemporary society we must ensure that we are always pragmatic, positive, and careful to avoid anything that may unsettle or disturb potential "clients." How unlike Jesus, who explains how it will be at the end of the age. Some will go away to eternal punishment and others to eternal life. These are

the words of the kindest shepherd who ever lived—
a shepherd who gave His life for the sheep.

> When the Son of Man comes in his glory, and all the
> angels with him, he will sit on his throne in heavenly
> glory. All the nations will be gathered before him, and
> he will separate the people one from another as a
> shepherd separates the sheep from the goats. He will
> put the sheep on his right and the goats on his left.
> (Matthew 25:31–33)

This is without question a sobering truth. As long
as preachers avoid it, listeners need not face it. But
we cannot at one and the same time ignore the fact
of God's judgment and make sense of the "big picture." In the same way that the Bible declares history to have a beginning, so we are told it is moving
toward a conclusion. The game does not go on in-
definitely; we are coming down to the final buzzer.

We are tempted to hope that our lives are akin to
a computer game. Sometimes when I travel, I fill in
odd moments by playing solitaire on my laptop
computer. (As long as no one looks over my shoulder I can give the impression of being hard at
work!) One of the options available to me at any
point is to press "reset." In doing so, I am dealt a
whole new hand and the game begins again. So it's
possible for me without facing ultimate defeat to
press "reset" when I get the first inkling that the
game does not appear to be going my way. Hin-
duism views the end of life as essentially the pressing of the reset button, and the law of karma will be
operative in our next attempt. Buddhism allows for
multiple resets as I go from incarnation to incarnation en route to Nirvana. Christianity has no such
feature. Christianity declares that history is not

cyclical but linear. It is moving to an end, and that end involves accountability. "We shall all answer for what we have done, and we shall all be judged either on the basis of our own righteousness (which will condemn us) or on the basis of the perfect righteousness of Him who is our Savior."[3] That we should be accepted at the bar of God's judgment on the basis of someone else's righteousness takes us again to the scandal of the previous chapter.

If we are going to face up to the straightforward statements of Scripture in relation to this matter, then we cannot avoid the staggering implication that our eternal destiny is involved. A God who is holy and just cannot let sin go unpunished. The Bible clearly teaches that there will be a division at the final judgment between those who are acquitted and those who are condemned. When the apostle Paul preached, this solemn truth was part of the key to his unashamed persuasiveness.

Held on house arrest and awaiting a public hearing, Paul was given the opportunity to speak to Felix, the Roman governor, in two hearings. In the second of these, Felix was accompanied by his wife, Drusilla (Acts 24:1–27). We should note that Drusilla had a reputation for her ravishing beauty, and Felix had seduced her from her rightful husband and taken her as his own. The couple was quite content to live within the framework of such lax moral standards. So, at their invitation, the apostle spoke to them about faith in Christ Jesus. When we consider the constituent elements of his sermon, we realize that this was no attempt on his part to tickle their ears or curry their favor.

His first point was *righteousness*. He must have told them about the holiness of God and how it is that men and women appear before Him as sinners. Perhaps he quoted the words of Psalm 11:7 (NASB): "For the Lord is righteous, He loves righteousness; the upright will behold His face." His second point was *self-control.* Imagine addressing the issue of passions and desires with a couple who were involved in an adulterous relationship. He may have quoted the words of Solomon: "Like a city whose walls are broken down is a man who lacks self-control" (Proverbs 25:28). And then he came to his third point, *the judgment to come.* Did he quote from Psalm 1: "The wicked will not stand in the judgment, nor sinners in the assembly of the righteous" (v. 5)? Or from Psalm 9:7: "The Lord reigns forever; he has established his throne for judgment"?

The result of his preaching, we are told, was that Felix was afraid and told him, "That's enough for now!" (Acts 24:25). How different this is from much of what we hear offered as the story of "faith in Christ Jesus" today. You may have, as a result of sermons you have heard, reached the conclusion that the matter of faith is, as we said in the opening chapter, entirely your own affair. You may have been living with the mistaken notion that "as long as you have faith, that's all that matters." But you have never to this point considered the *object* of faith as being the person of Jesus Christ and the *basis* of faith being what He has accomplished by His death on the cross. Jesus has been offered to you as One who can add to the sum of your total happiness. As a result, you do not know Him as a reality because you have never understood Him to be a necessity.

True Christianity confronts us with the bad news of our condition and the awesome prospect of judgment. It is only in light of these "dreadful" facts that the Good News of God's provision begins to shine like a light into our darkness. Why would anyone be so bold as to do what Paul did on that occasion? He actually tells us about his motivation in one of his letters: it is knowing the fear of the Lord which causes him to be so persuasive with people. It is on account of the fact that he is compelled by the love of Christ and convinced about the efficacy of the death of Christ that he is prepared to be regarded as even being "out of his mind."

> For Christ's love compels us, because we are convinced that one died for all, and therefore all died. And he died for all, that those who live should no longer live for themselves but for him who died for them and was raised again. (2 Corinthians 5:14–15)

This was not a matter of marginal importance but an issue of life and death, and as a result Paul was prepared to implore his readers to be reconciled to God. It is for the same reason that I would urge you to take this matter seriously.

"God has set a day." There is nothing uncertain about the fact of judgment. It is neither a random affair thrown up by chance nor an event driven by some blind, impersonal force. It will take place according to God's plan. It is not an illusion. It is factual. It will be perfectly fair, it will be dreadfully fearful, and it will be awfully final. All will be present; there will be no exemptions. No one will have anything to say in self-defense: all excuses will die upon our lips.

In the book of Revelation, the apostle John describes this dramatic scene.

Then I saw a great white throne and him who was seated on it. Earth and sky fled from his presence, and there was no place for them. And I saw the dead, great and small, standing before the throne, and books were opened. Another book was opened, which is the book of life. The dead were judged according to what they had done as recorded in the books. . . . If anyone's name was not found written in the book of life, he was thrown into the lake of fire. (Revelation 20:11–12, 15)

John does not say what "books were opened," but the context makes clear that they contain the records of our lives. They contain incontrovertible evidence of our guilt. There is no possibility of error in the celestial bookkeeping. The proof that the Judge of all the earth is doing right is all there in the books. We are about to conclude that our case is hopeless, for

If judgment were to proceed from those books alone there could be no hope for anyone. It is impossible to imagine anyone, anywhere, who could face an investigation in which every half-truth, every act of impatience, every unkindness, even every omission were indelibly, unfailingly recorded. It is simply impossible to imagine that the pathetic collection of really good deeds that I could muster in my defense could ever outweigh the mass of wrong acts of which I am undoubtedly guilty.[4]

Then we notice that there is "another book," which is set off from all the rest. In this book we find inscribed the names of those who have seen the futility of trying to establish their own goodness (as per the Pharisee in Jesus' story) and have (like the tax collector) cast themselves on God's mercy. The names in this book are still the names of sinners, but they belong to the company whose faith is in the Lamb of God who died in their place and bore their punishment. They stand before the Judge justified because their sinful souls are counted free on account of the sacrifice of a sinless Savior. In direct and chilling contrast, anyone whose name does not appear in the Book of Life will be thrown into the lake of fire. When the final audit takes place, men and women will either share in the blissful wonder of heaven or face the dreadful reality of hell.

If those whose names are written in the Book of Life will escape the judgment of condemnation on account of sin and may have complete confidence on the Day of Judgment, then surely it would make sense to discover how it is that one's name is entered in that book. Do not be misled into thinking of God as some kind of sentimental grandfather who is prepared, on account of weakness or laziness, to simply overlook the misdemeanors of His grandchildren. Payday is coming. God will settle the accounts. I read the story of a farmer who decided to challenge the God of Christianity. He hit on the idea of deliberately working on Sunday, the Christian day of rest and worship. After the September harvest he wrote to his local newspaper. "I plowed that field on Sunday, I sowed the grain on Sunday, I reaped it on Sunday. And I made greater profit on that field than on any other of my fields." The editor contented himself with a one-line response: *God doesn't settle His accounts in September.*

9

Forgiveness—
Friendship—
Focus

By now it should be clear that decisions we make in this life in relation to Jesus will have eternal consequences. "Whoever believes in the Son has eternal life, but whoever rejects the Son will not see life, for God's wrath remains on him" (John 3:36). We have seen that Christ came on a rescue mission. As we consider Him dying on the cross in the place of sinners, we realize that there in a moment in time we find heaven's love and heaven's justice meeting. As T. S. Mooney was fond of saying, "The grace of God reveals One who loves us so much as to have made Calvary possible, but who hates sin so much as to make Calvary necessary." When Jesus died as our substitute and received the wages of sin that we deserve, then the sins of all that will ever be pardoned were judged and punished, and it is on this basis that pardon is now offered to us as offenders.[1]

We have also seen that the heart of the human problem is our sin, on account of which we are objects of God's wrath. And this is not some arbitrary outburst on God's part. His wrath is His settled, inevitable reaction to unrighteousness. When Jesus bore the weight of our sins in His body on the cross, He was quenching God's wrath by obliterating our sins from His sight. It is only when we recognize this that we can then understand how it is that our fear, emptiness, stress, disappointment, and aloneness are symptoms of this deepest of all human problems. You may have "experimented" with Christianity as a means of dealing with some of those issues. You may even have enjoyed limited success in reducing stress or finding direction, but until you come to acknowledge your need of a Savior from sin you will never know the reality of taking hold of life that is truly life. What, then, are some of the benefits of the gospel?

FORGIVENESS

In Acts 10 is Luke's record of Peter's sermon in the home of Cornelius. During that sermon Peter provided a summary of the "good news of peace through Jesus Christ" (v. 36). In doing so, he explained the death and resurrection of Christ. Peter also pointed out that he and the other apostles received a divine commission to preach to the people. He made clear that he was not propounding some new speculative theory but, rather, a message that was in accord with what the Old Testament prophets had said. And at the very heart of the matter was forgiveness: "And all the prophets testify about him that everyone who believes in him receives forgiveness of sins through his name" (v. 43).

Unlike human forgiveness, which is often marked by reluctance, there is nothing grudging about the way in which God forgives. On account of the sacrifice of Jesus, which was adequate for the sins of all who would believe, the Father forgives all those who trust in the sacrifice of His Son. If we think about the record of our sins being stored in a computer, we might legitimately imagine the Father pressing the "delete" key and wiping out the record of our transgressions, once and for all.

The completeness of what God has done is graphically portrayed in the psalmist's words, "As far as the east is from the west, so far has he removed our transgressions from us" (Psalm 103:12). The prophet Micah asked the question, "Who is a God like you, who pardons sin?" (Micah 7:18). Then he described the full and generous forgiveness of God: "You will tread our sins underfoot and hurl all our iniquities into the depths of the sea" (v. 19). The promise of God through Jeremiah is "I will forgive their wickedness and will remember their sins no more" (Jeremiah 31:34). Here is the dramatic and wonderful news. When God forgives, not a single sin is left unforgiven. The debt of sin is completely wiped out, and the sinner's guilt is canceled.

In the 1970s, the late David Watson described how in speaking at an English university he had talked to one girl who had the reputation as "the toughest girl in the university." She had slept around freely and taken every drug on the campus. Outwardly she didn't care about anything and seemed quite hardened against the Christian faith. He recounted how, after one of his evangelistic talks, she came up to him, smoking a cigarette, to say that she had trusted Christ as her Savior and Lord. His immediate reaction: "Time will tell."

The next night she returned and he hardly recognized her as being the same person. She told how she'd spent most of the day crying. For years, she explained, in spite of her toughness and hardness, she felt deeply guilty. No one would have guessed it, but on that Sunday night all her guilt had been coming out and she was overwhelmed by the love of Jesus. She could not really believe that He loved her and had died for her and had taken away her sins. She found it incredible that God would forgive all her wickedness and keep no record of her wrongs.

And so the Word of God comes to troubled consciences, not to demoralize them, but instead to arouse them to their great need so that they will turn to the only One who can grant such complete and liberating forgiveness. This is what Shakespeare's Lady Macbeth was searching for but couldn't find. Although she has managed to cleanse her hands from the blood of her murderous act, she is unable to cleanse her conscience. And so she cries,

> Out, damned spot! Out, I say! . . . What, will these hands ne'er be clean? . . . Here's the smell of blood still: all the perfumes of Arabia will not sweeten this little hand.

She cannot live with herself, and her husband finds it increasingly difficult to live with her and so inquires of the doctor:

> Canst thou not minister to a mind diseased,
> Pluck from the memory a rooted sorrow,
> Raze out the written troubles of the brain,
> And with some sweet oblivious antidote
> Cleanse the stuff'd bosom of the perilous stuff
> Which weighs upon the heart?

The physician's reply expresses the ultimate frustration of modern psychiatry in its attempts to deal with real guilt: "Therein the patient must minister to himself" (*Macbeth* 5.1.39–58; 5.3.40–46).

If you are aware of sins that lie on your conscience and you long to be "set free," then you need to be honest enough to face up to your condition and turn to the only place where sins are washed away and burdens are lifted and new starts are possible: the cross of the Lord Jesus Christ.

The worst thing you can do is try to hide by blaming it all on someone or something else. When I was assistant to Derek Prime in Edinburgh in the middle seventies, I had the privilege of doing a considerable amount of pastoral visitation. Part of my list was comprised of individuals, who for periods of time, were patients in psychiatric wards. On a couple of occasions I attended a forum of doctors, social workers, and clergy. It quickly became apparent that the underlying philosophy was one that encouraged the patients to externalize any notions of guilt. This perspective is aptly summarized in Anna Russell's "Psychiatric Folk Song":

> I went to my psychiatrist to be psychoanalyzed
> To find out why I killed the cat and blacked my
>   husband's eye.
> He laid me on a downy couch to see what he could find,
> And here's what he dredged up, from my subconscious
>   mind.
> When I was one, my mummy hid my dolly in a trunk
> And so it follows, naturally, that I am always drunk.
> When I was two, I saw my father kiss the maid one day,
> And that is why I suffer from kleptomania.
> At three I had a feeling of ambivalence towards my
>   brothers

> And so it follows naturally I poisoned all my lovers.
> But I am happy now I have learned the lessons this
>   has taught:
> Everything I do that's wrong, is someone else's fault!

In direct contrast, the Bible encourages us to face up to our condition, to say with the young man in the story of the Father's love in Luke 15, "I have sinned against heaven and against you" (v. 18). That young man went on to discover a depth of grace and mercy he knew he did not deserve but certainly required.

I recall the experience as a schoolboy of having my name put up on the blackboard as a result of my misdemeanors. Sometimes my name appeared as early as Monday morning. I then had to live the rest of the week with the realistic sense of guilt that was heightened each time I looked to see my name. What a wonderful, liberating experience it was when the teacher took the duster and cleaned the blackboard. She wiped the record clean and in doing so eased my troubled conscience. In a far greater way, the Bible tells us that the blood of Christ clears the debt, erases the transgression, and declares a fresh start. This does not put the reconciled sinner in a position where he no longer sins. But as he confesses his sins, he finds that God is utterly reliable and straightforward and forgives our sins and makes us thoroughly clean from all that is evil.

FRIENDSHIP

As we have already seen, one of the unsavory features of our society is a sense of aloneness that can be experienced even when we are surrounded by people. Jung suggested that emptiness was the central neurosis of our time. Insofar as men and women are first alienated from God and consequently from each other, Jung touches on the truth. We receive mail from people we have never met, and despite their attempts to make us feel attached, the reality of our disengagement is hard to disguise. How are we supposed to feel when we receive letters which begin:

Dear 00045-68-GHJ,
We have a *personal* interest in your welfare . . .

One way to try to deal with this is to deny any need of friendship at all, to take the approach that says, "I am a rock, an island," and to despise friendship as yielding only pain and heartache.

In direct contrast to that cynicism, most people would agree with the ancient observation,

Poor is the friendless master of a world;
A world in purchase for a friend is gain.

In 1983, Professor Eugene Kennedy of Loyola University gave an interview to *U.S. News and World Report* entitled "Why a Good Friend Is Hard to Find." In the course of that interview, he made this telling observation:

There is a profound longing for friendship, a poignant searching for the kinds of things that only close and lasting relationships give you. . . .

What people are looking for in life is someone to whom they can tell the story of their lives. That's why there arc ham-radio operators. Why do they send out those signals into the night? Their reward is being able to say, "Somebody in Anchorage heard me last night." We are all looking for someone who will pick up our signal and listen.

People want the rewards of friendship without the hazards of friendship, but you can't have one without the other. There's a death involved in every true act of friendship.[2]

That last sentence leads us naturally to Jesus, who was called the friend of sinners and by whose death friendship with God has become a realistic possibility.

Greater love has no one than this, that he lay down his life for his friends. You are my friends if you do what I command. . . . You did not choose me, but I chose you. (John 15:13–14, 16)

This friendship is marked by *the initiative of Jesus*. Unlike human friendships, which result from mutual choice, Jesus says that friendship with Him is one-sided in its origin. It was customary in the time of Jesus for serious students to seek out a teacher of their choice. Here, in John, we are reminded that the seeking begins with God. When the wonder of this grips our minds, then we will be struck by the security that it brings. The hymn writer summarized it like this:

> *I've found a Friend, oh, such a Friend!*
> *He loved me ere I knew Him;*
> *He drew me with the cords of love,*
> *And thus He bound me to Him.*
> *And round my heart so closely twine*

Those ties which naught can sever,
For I am His, and He is mine,
Forever and forever.

This friendship is also marked by *intimacy with Jesus.* Jesus distinguishes between the kind of instruction a master gives to his servants (which is usually without explanation as to why or wherefore) and the relationship of friendship by which we become His confidants. The mutual affection the friends of Jesus are in turn to express toward each other is on account of Christ's display of friendship toward them. His example of self-sacrificing love is to be the pattern of their love for each other.

This is actually more than friendship—it's *family.* We all know the old adage, "You can choose your friends, but you can't choose your family." That is certainly true of God's family. But this is one of the great benefits of the gospel. We have been called into a great company of people who are united by the fact that we have been "made . . . alive with Christ," "by grace . . . saved," "created in Christ Jesus to do good works," and "brought near through the blood of Christ" (Ephesians 2:5, 8, 10, 13). Although we were formerly "without hope and without God in the world" (v. 12), alienated from God at the deepest possible level, now it has all changed. "You are no longer foreigners and aliens," Paul told the Ephesians, "but fellow citizens with God's people and members of God's household" (v. 19).

Our relationships are flavored by a common experience of *love,* as we have already seen. But also by a shared discovery of *peace.* Our guilty past has been canceled; we are no longer rebels in arms. Not only is there a sense of forgiveness, but there is an accompanying access into God's presence. When I go to my father's home in Yorkshire, I enjoy the privileges of unlimited access and a wonderful sense of peace in his presence and in the company of my sisters. To a far greater degree we enjoy this experience in our heavenly Father's presence. Remember how this was never the case until that large curtain was torn from top to bottom, declaring the way open to peace. Equally we experience the benefit of realistic *joy*. This, of course, does not mean being removed from the realm of difficulty or even tragedy. But it does mean that even in disappointment and pain we recognize that our heavenly Father is using each of these experiences to cultivate our character and to allow us to discover that ultimately our only true source of joy is God Himself.

For some this may appear to represent an insurmountable challenge. "How am I going to manage to do all this?" "I'm not sure that I will be able to keep producing all this love, joy, and peace that you are talking about." Exactly! You won't! But this is the best of news. When we cast ourselves upon God's mercy, not only are we put in a right relationship with God but we also receive a "new life" by the power of the Holy Spirit. Jesus spoke about this in terms of receiving the gift of the Holy Spirit. This is not something remote, nor to be regarded as weird. The Christian life is not a call to try to fulfill very high standards by our own effort. There is no question that crowds of well-meaning but sad souls believe that to be the case. For them, Christianity is an ethical system we must apply ourselves to with as much endeavor as we can muster. Consequently, they stumble from failure to failure; and the harder they try, the worse it all becomes. The power for living the Christian life comes from God.

> The power of the Spirit means that the individual is able to achieve what was impossible before. Imagine an old car making its way up a steep hill, hardly making the grade. With a look of pity you overtake it quickly. The next week you see it in front of you again. *I'll overtake it,* you think to yourself. But as soon as you try, you find you cannot! A transformation in performance has taken place because the car has a new engine. It has power to lead a new life.[3]

It is this new life that brings with it an appetite for the food of God's Word, a sincere desire for the company of other family members, and a willingness to serve on the basis of the gifts and abilities we have been given.

This experience of life will not be marred by death. We will simply relocate and pick up, in a more wonderful way than we can imagine, from where we left off. The friendship we enjoy is not going to end at a moment in time but will instead last for all of eternity.

FOCUS

A world without God is a world without meaning. An absence of purpose is one of the largest contributing factors to the experience of depression. If the universe sprang from nothing and will ultimately return to nothing, we have no answer to the "Why?" and meaninglessness becomes the only incontrovertible knowledge available to us. This sense of futility is not the exclusive domain of the departments of philosophy in our universities. Lee Iococca, who masterminded one of the great turn-around stories of American business and shared in the financial windfall it created, was asked if he had an answer to the purpose of life. He replied, "As I start my twilight years, I still do not know. All I know is, fame and fortune are for the birds." Similarly, when Mike Wallace of *60 Minutes* asked the billionaire Robert Maxwell, "When will enough be enough?" Maxwell responded, "There will never be enough. That is the purposelessness of life."

Now the Christian life is set in direct contrast to this. When Jesus called His first disciples, it was not to wander aimlessly on some religious trek. Rather, He called them to deny themselves, to refuse to look back, and to follow Him along the narrow road of radical discipleship. This story needs to be heard. So many members of Generation X have dismissed Christianity without ever having considered the claims of Christ. They have been put off by encountering a pale imitation of the real thing. What they need to encounter are lives that have been totally transformed by the power of Jesus Christ. A life like that of Jim Elliot. A life of passionate devotion to the cause of Christ. A life cut short by the very people to whom he had gone to tell about Jesus. On Sunday, January 8, 1956, Jim and his four companions were killed by Auca Indians. Six years earlier, Jim had made an entry in his daily journal: "God, I pray you, light these idle sticks of my life and may I burn for you. Consume my life, my God, for it is yours. I seek not a long life, but a full one, like you, Lord Jesus."

In writing thus, he was following the pattern of another martyr who had blazed the trail of living with purpose. When Paul wrote from a Roman jail to his friends in Philippi, he explained, "But one thing I do: Forgetting what is behind and straining toward what is ahead, I press on toward the goal to win the prize for which God has called me heavenward in Christ Jesus" (Philippians 3:13–14).

Like a runner in a race, he is focused. His aim is definite and well defined. He permits nothing to divert him from his course. He has one thing in mind. There is something very attractive about such a singular focus. The late Harvey Penick, golf teacher from Austin, Texas, worked with many champions throughout the years, among them, Tom Kite and Ben Crenshaw. Part of his genius as a teacher would seem to have been in his ability to express himself clearly and succinctly. He once wrote:

> I would approach my college players before a match and tell them one thing: *Take dead aim.* This is a wonderful thought to keep in mind all the way round the course, not just on the first tee. . . . I can't say it too many times. It's the most important advice in this book. *Take dead aim.* Make it a point to do it every time on every shot. Don't just do it from time to time, when you happen to remember. *Take dead aim.*[4]

In terms of the Christian life, Paul was doing just that. He shut out all distracting thoughts. That was what he meant by "forgetting" certain things. He was obviously not about to forget God's goodness to him in the past, nor the valuable lessons he was learning on the journey. But there were recollections from his pre-Christian life (as there will be for us) that held the potential for discouragement. So he resolved not to allow temptations succumbed to in the past, or disappointments, to defeat him. Nor would he let encouragements he had known to induce slackness or smugness. The fact that he had tripped on "lap 3" or that he had run with ease on "lap 9" must not interfere with his single-minded pursuit of the tape.

This is the Christian life. Think of the various aspects of your life—social, emotional, intellectual, relational, physical—as spokes in a wheel. Unless each spoke is firmly anchored in the hub, it will swing aimlessly connected at the rim. When our focus is on "winning the prize," this pleases God and we are transformed. We are tempted to try and settle all the issues of our lives, and *then* we will get to the "hub question." But it must happen in reverse. First we must have an unashamed commitment to head for the goal, and *then* the issues of career and marriage and the challenges of failure or success will begin to fall in line. When Paul wrote a letter to his friends in Colossae, he described the supremacy of Jesus, and in the course of that discussion, made this staggering statement: "He [Christ] is before all things, and in him all things hold together" (Colossians 1:17).

You may be feeling right now that your life is absent any sense of cohesion. You fill up your days with activity, and yet you are devoid of any overarching sense of purpose. You are asking yourself what life is all about, and you wonder whether all that matters is the moment. You may even have begun to "believe" some of what we have been considering, but you are unsure just how to make it personal. There is clearly a difference between a working knowledge of the train timetable and the experience of making a journey. You may be familiar with the menu in a local restaurant without eating the food. You can even become a waiter and never eat what you serve. In the same way, you may have begun to teach in the Sunday school at your church. The children are all ears as you tell them about Jesus, the Bread of Life. And you offer to them what you have never tasted yourself. We must then consider what is involved in moving from assent to commitment.

10

Coming to Christt

T he question before us in this chapter is this: How do the benefits we've been considering become ours? Or, how does this "true Christianity" become "my" Christianity? Or, how do I come to know what angels wish they knew? Since much of what we will consider may appear to be formulaic, it is important at the outset to acknowledge the *mystery* which surrounds this. When Jesus was talking with Nicodemus about being born again, He referred to this factor. "The wind blows where it likes, you can hear the sound of it but you have no idea where it comes from and where it goes. Nor can you tell how a man is born by the wind of the Spirit" (John 3:8 PHILLIPS). The hymn writer expresses the same thought in poetry:

> *I know not how the Spirit moves,*
> *Convincing men of sin,*
> *Revealing Jesus through the Word,*
> *Creating faith in Him.*

This is not to say that we cannot understand the steps involved but it is to recognize the amazing wonder of God's grace whereby Jesus, as with Zacchaeus, comes to where I am, calls me by my name, and changes me. So we note that this life-changing encounter takes place both mysteriously and individually. Before we go any further in thinking about how this can be your experience, here are two stories by way of illustration.

For a brief period in 1975 I had the opportunity to help a newfound Japanese friend, Masinobu, with his pronunciation of English. When we met he was a professor of law in a Japanese university. As we became friends, he told me his story. He was the third of nine children. His father was an officer in the Japanese army during the Second World War. At age twelve he went to live in a Buddhist temple in the prospect of one day becoming a priest. Finding no satisfaction, he returned to his home until graduation from high school. A bright student, with a black belt in judo, he began work in Osaka to help the family finances. He spent his evenings going to parties and getting drunk. Stalled in the laboratory where he was working, he took a job washing dishes in a hotel in the evenings to fund his university studies until a grant became available.

The philosophies of Hegel, Schopenhauer, and Nietzsche rattled his convictions, and not only did he go on to postgraduate study in the philosophy of law in Tokyo, but he also became an avowed communist. He was a student leader in the anti-American riots of 1969. Believing that the best way to change man was by politics, he determined that he would become a university professor. To stay out of jail in Japan, he went to study in Germany. "I had no friends, and I was very lonely. I saw no reason or purpose in life; I had no hope for the future; I couldn't find the truth; neither did I want to live any more. I wanted to kill myself."

Out walking one Sunday morning, he heard the peal of the church bells that seemed to summon him to a consideration of the claims of Christianity. It so happened that around this time he was invited for a meal at the home of a family that turned out to be Christian. Intrigued by what they were saying, but unable to read the German Bible they gave him, he had his father send him a Japanese Bible, which he began to read. There was about it, he said, something that began to ring true. He described the evening when, out of the blue, "all my past sins rose up and confronted me—the fights I had been in, the people I had attacked. A whole catalogue of sins came, as it were, before my eyes, and it broke upon me that I was a sinner before God and needed His forgiveness. I saw that I could never work my way to heaven by all that I had been doing and that only because Christ had died for my sins on the cross was this forgiveness possible." And then he concluded, "I have found that Jesus is the absolute truth—God's truth revealed in human form—and He is the Son of God. . . . I have found a peace and joy which I never knew previously. I now know that life is not meaningless. I have found what Buddhism and Communism can never give—a new life and a changed heart."

The second story comes from a young couple who were in our church for a while before employment took them to Florida. I hesitate to use this because of the personal references, but I think the potential benefit outweighs the risk. This is part of their Christmas letter.

Randy and I are rejoicing this Christmas because of the real joy of Christmas. 1995 was a tough year for us, but few would know from looking at our lives. We both had great jobs and income from a worldly perspective, a new home, and many opportunities. Someone once said, "The smallest package in the world is someone wrapped up in himself." Sadly, we were probably the smallest packages in the world. We were caught in the "me," "self-esteem" movement and thought happiness lay in meeting our own needs and desires. These ideas were highlighted to us each day by the covers of magazines and movies. The path of self-gratification proved to be meaningless to us both, and we were still searching for fulfillment and happiness.

We stumbled upon a church with a pastor who taught the love of God the Father directly from the Bible. He taught us the person and character of God, not a bunch of rules that is so common in religion today. Both of us having gone to West Point, we were pretty good at following rules. You can fool a lot of people by following rules and looking good, but you can't fool yourself or God. The guilt was still there, even though the world told us not to feel guilty. That is why this short, skinny pastor's message was so compelling. Could the words of the Bible be true? Was there really a God who knew us personally and cared enough to know all the tiny details of our lives? Was the Bible really the inerrant Word of God or just a collection of stories from half-crazed, unpopular Jews? This supernatural phenomenon is not unlike the story in the first Star Trek *movie when the bald girl goes looking for her creator, Vyger. These were all the questions we sought to answer.*

We found the answer; I in October of 1995, and Randy on December 26, 1995. The verse that sent the message home for Randy was Proverbs 19:3: "A man's own folly ruins his life, yet his heart rages against the Lord." For me it was Psalm 40:2: "He lifted me out of the slimy pit, out of the mud and mire; he set my feet on a rock and gave me a firm place to stand."

This reconciliation with God would not be possible without the love of God. He made the first move because He loved us first. Romans 5:6 tells us, "You see, at just the right time, when we were still powerless, Christ died for the ungodly." And Romans 5:8 says, "But God demonstrates his own love for us in this: While we were still sinners, Christ died for us." We celebrate Christmas because we know that "God so loved the world that he gave his one and only Son, that whoever believes in him, shall not perish but have eternal life" (John 3:16).

These two stories, one of a communist from the sixties and the other of two materialists from the nineties, serve to illustrate the way in which God moves mysteriously and individually.

Now, what about you, the reader? I hope these accounts leave you in no doubt that genuine Christian faith is more than being prepared to say, "I believe there is a God." Or even being able to say, "I believe that Jesus is who He claimed to be." That is an essential part of faith, but by itself it is inadequate. After all, as James the brother of Jesus tells us, even demons are orthodox when it comes to this, but they clearly are not Christians (James

2:19)! Faith involves more than just an *assent* to certain facts. It means *accepting* that the facts I affirm can be trusted. But it also means that I am prepared to act upon what I believe to be true.

Perhaps a simple analogy will help. When I was a small boy, I often traveled the city of Glasgow with my grandfather. The city is divided north from south by the River Clyde. Today there are a number of bridges across the river. Forty years ago there were fewer bridges and access was provided by ferries: a large one that transported cars and "the wee ferry" for people. Now, imagine that I arrived at the Clydeside to await the arrival of the ferry. Not only did I believe that it existed, I declared my trust in the ferry master to take me safely to the other side. But the fact remains that I would never have known what it was to make the journey unless I had been prepared to "get on board."

So I may believe that God promises me forgiveness of sins. I may declare my willingness to trust that promise; but until I respond, I shall not obtain forgiveness.

Alister McGrath uses another analogy which you may find more helpful.

> Consider a bottle of penicillin, the famous antibiotic identified by Alexander Fleming, and first produced for clinical use at the Radcliffe Infirmary, Oxford, and responsible for saving the lives of countless individuals who would otherwise have died from various forms of blood poisoning. Imagine that—
> a. this bottle is sitting on my bedside table, and that—
> b. I am suffering from blood poisoning.

What are my options?
    a. I may *accept* that this bottle of penicillin exists.
    b. I may *trust* that it is capable of curing my ill-
       ness, which otherwise will probably kill me.
       But I shall never cure my blood poisoning,
       unless—
    c. I *act* upon that trust and take the penicillin.
       Acceptance and trust prepare the way for the
       final component of faith—entering into the
       promise and receiving what it offers. I may
       accept that the bottle exists, and I may trust in
       its ability to cure blood poisoning—but unless I
       take the drug which it contains, I have not ben-
       efited from my faith in it. I shall die, accepting
       and trusting, but having failed to benefit at all
       from the resource which could have saved me.[1]

When John wrote about believing in Jesus, he talked at the same time of receiving Him. He was making the point that these "are different ways of looking at the same spiritual change wherein a man ceases to rely on his own merits and achievements and puts his trust in Christ instead," as Leon Morris put it.[2] The emphasis was not upon simply believing that what He says is true, but actually trusting Him as a person. So, for example, when Jesus issued the wonderful invitation recorded in Matthew 11:28–30 for all "who are weary and burdened" to come to Him, then come we must. To stand at the other side of the street, as it were, burdened by our guilt and sin and saying to ourselves, "That sounds like it may be right," is not the same as falling down before Him and casting all our burdens at His feet.

On two classic occasions Peter and Paul respectively were asked point-blank about making the transition from assent to commitment: "What are we supposed to do?" Each time they responded in a way that was clear and concise, and the lives of men and women were changed for good. "Repent and be baptized, every one of you, in the name of Jesus Christ for the forgiveness of your sins " (Acts 2:38). "Believe in the Lord Jesus, and you will be saved" (Acts 16:31).

In drawing this chapter to a close, I want to emulate their example, and in doing so my indebtedness to men like Michael Green and the late David Watson will be impossible to conceal. Their clear, quiet, confident directions to "seekers" have strongly influenced my own approach to spiritual midwifery!

THERE IS SOMETHING TO ADMIT

There are actually quite a number of things to admit, but they all eventually boil down to the basic fact that I am a sinner. I have broken God's law. As we saw in chapter 3, each of us has failed miserably when it comes to keeping His commandments. We haven't honored our parents as we should; we have tolerated untruthfulness; we have been envious of our neighbors; and while we may not have actually committed murder, we have tolerated murderous thoughts. In some cases our lives have been lived in active rebellion against God, while others of us have adopted a posture of casual neglect. So whether in defiance or indifference, we have lived our lives consistently leaving God out of the equation.

It is important to recognize that our natural tendency is not to acknowledge our sin. We are, as we have seen, far more prone to blame our circumstances or our genes. We are keen to justify ourselves and to gain some comfort in the assurance that we are not as bad as some people we know. So what brings us to the place where we know that we must admit, in the words of the young man in Luke 15, that "I have sinned against heaven and against you" (vv. 18, 21)? The answer is that this is something God does. Jesus explained to His disciples that He would send the Holy Spirit: "When he comes, he will convince the world of the meaning of sin, of true goodness and of judgment" (John 16:8 PHILLIPS). This "conviction" is not something we ourselves create. By ourselves we may be prepared to acknowledge that we are "fed up with things," or that we have "failed to reach our goals," or that we have "let ourselves down." Such expressions, in and of themselves, convey the fact that we feel sorry for ourselves but not that we are sorry for our sins. The prodigal in the pigsty was hungry and friendless and broke. His circumstances provided an occasion for self-pity. But he was not crying because of the pleasures he had lost. When he "came to his senses," he admitted his sin. So we see that this total reversal in the way we think about ourselves and our sin is as a result of the Spirit of God convincing us of truth we have been working hard to avoid.

We should not get tied up in seeking to determine how much "conviction" is required. Some people hurry to the doctor at the first sign of disease, while others wait until their condition is grave before seeking help. So it is in coming to Christ. Degrees of conviction will differ, but whether the depth and length of conviction is small or great, we will be brought to the place where we admit our sin. It has been said that there are ultimately only two things necessary for us to know if we are to become Christians: first, that I am a great sinner; and second, that Christ is a great Savior. This brings us to the next step in the process.

THERE IS SOMETHING TO BELIEVE

In a nutshell it is this: Jesus is the only Savior from the sin to which I have just admitted. We may have begun our journey fairly convinced that Jesus was simply a "good man." But as we considered the evidence, we were forced in a different direction. Our skepticism was dealt a healthy blow as we examined the Resurrection, and we have found that there is a sense in which we are coming to believe against our wishes. We certainly did not set out predisposed to believe. And so we find ourselves agreeing with this statement:

> Faith is *forced* consent. That is to say, when evidence is judged by the mind to be sufficient, the state of mind we call "faith" is the inevitable effect. . . . Whenever the reasons are judged sufficient, faith or belief is induced.[3]

So we come to believe that God has made provision for our sin in the person of His Son. "We see real love, not in the fact that we loved God, but that he loved us and sent his Son to make personal atonement for our sins" (1 John 4:10 PHILLIPS). It is through the Cross that God pardons those who believe in Christ. Without this, we would be shut out from His presence forever. I can recall the wonder of this gripping me in my preteens on a Sunday afternoon in Glasgow while attending Bible class. About 120 boys were singing heartily:

There's a way back to God, from the dark paths of sin;
There's a door that is open and you may go in.
At Calvary's cross, that's where you begin,
When you come as a sinner to Jesus.

It is by the Cross that God displays and satisfies His perfect and holy justice by executing the punishment our sins deserve. Although this may appear foolishness to some and cause others to stumble, God's wisdom is set forward in the death of His Son. Again, the hymn writer captures so much in few words. Writing of the Cross, he says:

O safe and happy shelter,
O refuge tried and sweet.
O trysting place where heaven's love
And heaven's justice meet.

We are only a few paragraphs away from recognizing that when it comes to faith there is something that we must do. "*We* believe in Christ, and God does not and cannot believe for us."[4] Having said that, we are forced again to consider the "mystery" whereby the Spirit of God not only convinces us of our sin so that we will *admit* to it, but also creates faith in Jesus so that we will *believe* in Him.

John Stott says: "We must never think of salvation as a kind of transaction between God and us in which He contributes grace and we contribute faith. For we were dead and had to be quickened before we could believe."[5] Sinclair Ferguson says: "The faith with which we believe and trust is only ours because God has created it within our hearts. When we find ourselves saying, 'Lord, I believe, help my unbelief,' then we have reached another landmark in the outworking of God's plan of salvation."[6]

THERE IS SOMETHING TO CONSIDER

Although no analogy is perfect, I have found the marriage ceremony and marriage itself as a helpful picture of at least part of what is involved in becoming a Christian. We will return to this under the next heading, but I mention it now for this reason: No matter how well prepared a couple may be for marriage, there is no way for them to realize the cost involved in remaining true to their vows as they make their journey through life. The unreserved commitment to live together "for better, for worse; for richer, for poorer" will be as costly as it is rewarding. So before a couple dash down the aisle in a great surge of emotion, we need to remind them that marriage is not to be entered upon lightly or carelessly but thoughtfully with due consideration of the purposes of God. To a far greater and more significant extent, we need to come to terms with the cost involved in following the Lord Jesus. Listen to the way He put it:

> If anyone wants to follow in my footsteps, he must give up all right to himself, carry his cross every day and keep close behind me. For the man who wants to save his life will lose it, but the man who loses his life for my sake will save it. (Luke 9:23–24 PHILLIPS)

Now be careful not to misunderstand this. We are not backtracking on what we have already said, namely, that the only thing we "contribute" to our salvation is the sin from which we need to be saved.

The way in which I learned the important distinction was by remembering that while *entrance* to the Christian life is *free,* the *annual subscription* is *everything I have!* There is a cost involved in . . .

Saying No to Sin

When Jesus began to preach, His early sermons were short and to the point. For example:

> The time has come. . . The kingdom of God is near. Repent and believe the good news! (Mark 1:15)

> Come, follow me, . . . and I will make you fishers of men. (Matthew 4:19)

Notice that His first call is to repentance. At its simplest, this means to turn *from* sin *to* God. It does not mean that we simply recognize sin for what it is. It is more than a sense of remorse. It involves a change of heart and mind that results in a change of direction. As we have seen, the experience and depth of emotion in repentance will be different from person to person, but there are certain characteristics which Sinclair Ferguson points out as being commonly present in all repentance.

1. A sense of shame.

This is illustrated in Psalm 51 when David cries to the Lord after he had committed adultery with Bathsheba. "For I know my transgressions, and my sin is always before me. Against you, you only, have I sinned and done what is evil in your sight" (Psalm 51:3–4). We can almost see him, bowing low, daring hardly to look up and unable and unwilling to disguise his disgrace.

2. This leads to *humbling*.

Instead of jumping to our defense or trying to blame our actions on people or circumstances, we acknowledge our accountability and find voice in the words of the tax collector, "God, have mercy on me, a sinner" (Luke 18:13).

3. There is an accompanying sense of *sorrow* and *regret*.

When the prodigal put his head on the pillow on his first evening back home, when the sounds of the party had faded and he looked across the room at his new robe and fine shoes discarded on his chair, and he rolled his ring around his finger, do you think he was missing the "far country"? No! I think if we could have sat quietly concealed in the corner of his room, we would have heard the sobs and seen the tears and watched in wonder as he knelt by his bed and mourned over the wasted years and the squandered privileges. The memory of sin is distasteful to the truly penitent.

4. There is also a *recognition of God's pardon*.

It is the kindness of God that leads us to repentance (Romans 2:4). When the truth of God's Word has cut to the core of my rebellious heart and exposed my guilt, then "grace appears on the horizon offering forgiveness, and the sunshine of the love of God melts my heart and draws me back to Him."[7]

While we are emphasizing the need for repentance at the gateway of faith, it would be wrong for us to think of it as an isolated instance at the beginning of the Christian life. This is something which continues through our entire life. When Martin

Luther nailed his Ninety-five Theses on the door of the Wittenberg church, the top of the list was: "Our Lord and Master Jesus Christ, in saying 'Repent ye' . . . intended that the whole of the life of believers should be repentance."

Saying No to Self

What we mean by this is simply that Christ comes first, before everything and everyone else. This has a peculiarly challenging ring in the midst of a culture that has gone to great lengths to bolster self-esteem and make much of the individual. When Jesus told His would-be followers about the need to *deny* themselves, He was making it clear that He is not only a perfect Savior but also Sovereign Lord. There isn't room on the throne for two. He is the One who rules over every department of our lives. This means that my time and my talents and my relationships and my career will all be brought under His jurisdiction. For the early Christians who lived in the Roman Empire this was a radical prospect. How could they honestly declare that "Caesar is Lord" when their allegiance was to the lordship of Jesus Christ? Removed as we are by time and geography from the demands of the Roman Empire, we still face the temptation to bow down to other idols and lords. Saying no to self will mean denying myself to myself. The Christian's perspective on life is the absolute antithesis of the attitude expressed in William E. Henley's famous boast,

> It matters not how strait the gate,
> How charged with punishments the scroll.
> I am the master of my fate:
> I am the captain of my soul.

The Christian understands that life is lived in dependence upon Jesus and on a daily basis he renews his unconditional surrender to Him. Consider how Dietrich Bonhoeffer expressed this in *The Cost of Discipleship:*

> The cross is laid on every Christian. The first Christ-suffering which every man must experience is the call to abandon the attachments of this world. It is that dying of the old man which is the result of his encounter with Christ. As we embark upon discipleship we surrender ourselves to Christ in union with his death—we give our lives to death. Thus it begins; the cross is not the terrible end to an otherwise God-fearing and happy life, but it meets us at the beginning of our communion with Christ. When Christ calls a man, he bids him come and die.[8]

Saying No to Secrecy

A few years ago my wife and I had the privilege of spending an evening in the company of Professor Tom Sutherland, who had been one of the hostages held for years by terrorists in Beirut. As we listened to him tell the story of captivity and then liberation it was clear that he was thrilled with his freedom and glad of every opportunity to tell others just what it meant to him. When a man or woman discovers the freedom that Jesus brings, then they will be ready and willing to let others know. The Bible confirms this in a number of places. "If you confess with your mouth, 'Jesus is Lord,' and believe in your heart that God raised Him from the dead, you will be saved" (Romans 10:9; cf. Matthew 10:32; Luke 12:8; 1 John 4:15).

When we noted earlier the response of Peter to the question of the crowd, we saw that he urged them to first of all repent and then be baptized. In doing the latter they were saying farewell to any notion of secret discipleship. The Jews regarded baptism as being necessary only for Gentile converts, and so for them to undergo the humiliation of declaring their submission to Jesus in this radical fashion was a clear expression of their faith. While coming to trust in Christ is undoubtedly a personal matter, it is not at the same time private. An unbaptized Christian is like a soldier without a uniform or a husband who refuses to wear a wedding ring.

THERE IS SOMETHING TO DO

In one sense this should already be clear as a result of what we have considered under the other headings. Just in case we did not fully grasp what we said about repentance, here is the definition that is found in the Westminster Shorter Catechism: "Repentance unto life is a saving grace, whereby a sinner out of a true sense of his sin, and apprehension of the mercy of God in Christ, does with grief and hatred of his sin, turn from it unto God with full purpose of, and endeavor after, new obedience."

Notice that there is a turning *from* and a turning *to*.

We have noted the progression that is involved in personal faith. We come to accept certain facts concerning Jesus—He is the expected Messiah; He is Savior and Lord. But mere mental assent to these facts without any corresponding action no more brings us to personal faith than memorizing a menu allows us to enjoy a meal. True faith means moving beyond the awareness of the existence of our Lord and Savior Jesus Christ to a living, personal relationship with Him.

As we have read or heard the Bible preached, we have discovered something we never knew possible. As the facts have been presented to us, the Holy Spirit has been convincing us of their truth. It is in this way that we have become convinced that the fundamental problem we face is the fact of our inherent sinfulness. The more we have read, the clearer it has become that Jesus is the solution to our problem. Gradually, or in some cases suddenly, the Good News dawns upon us and we become aware of the fact that faith has come about, not as a result of clever arguments, but through the power of the Holy Spirit.

To come back to the marriage analogy with which we began, we might think of becoming a Christian in these terms. Although the marriage ceremony itself is relatively brief and certainly to the point, there is usually a significant period of discovery before the knot is tied. There is also, God willing, a long journey of growing and deepening love that follows the exchange of rings. But at the heart of the matter there is a question to be answered by both parties: "Do you take this woman to be your lawful wedded wife?" It is always of interest to me that there is no question which tackles the issue of feelings. The whole matter is related to the mind and will. Not that emotion is absent, but that it is not the basis of either the question or the answer. And so it follows that two separate individuals are united in a moment in time; and as a result of their union, life will never be the same again! If I may suggest, without any loss of wonder or reverence and without undermining all that we have already said about the nature of saving faith, this gives us a picture of what it means for us to trust in Christ.

Imagine that you are standing side by side with the Lord Jesus at the end of the aisle and before the gaze of God the Father. The Father then addresses His Son. "Do you take this sinner?" To which the Son replies, "I do, Father; I died in his place that he might be forgiven." And then the Father addresses you with the question: "Do you take this Savior?"

Before you say, "I do," there will probably be a whole variety of thoughts and questions clamoring for your attention as you prepare to say these two life-changing words.

- Are you not struck by the wonder of God's initiative in finding you and calling your name and making such a proposal?
- Do not be misled by thinking that someone else can answer for you. As surely as Jesus called Zacchaeus by name, so He addresses you.
- Recognize that the question is addressed to your will and not to your emotions.
- Nothing else can take the place of this moment of commitment. There are many religious people, well-versed in the Bible, keen on ceremony, and concerned for the well-being of others, but they have never said, "I do."
- Do not stay away for fear that you are not "good enough" for such a relationship. It is the very absence of our goodness and fitness which makes the invitation so wonderful.
- Do not allow anyone or anything to divert your gaze from the loveliness of Christ.
- Do not delay!

If God has shown you your need and given you this desire, then you must forsake everything and trust Christ, *now!* It is possible to find yourself in a familiar cycle. You hear God's Word explained, or you read material like this book, and as a result you make the decision to "shape up." So instead of turning to Christ and accepting what He has done on our behalf, you commence religious exercises. You avoid certain activities you consider questionable and embrace others that appear desirable. And within a short while it all fizzles out. That's because you are trying to achieve by an external routine what can only be accomplished by a personal relationship.

It is imperative that you face the urgency of this issue. There's a time coming when it will all be too late. One of the saddest examples of this is Herod. He had a deep respect for John the Baptist, and "he used to listen to him and be profoundly disturbed, and yet he enjoyed hearing him" (Mark 6:20 PHILLIPS). Herod had apparently developed his own routine. He was genuinely interested in what John had to say. He made some minor adjustments to his way of life on the strength of what he heard. But eventually he capitulated to the pressure of the crowd and had his preacher beheaded. Pilate is another individual who could not handle the peer pressure when it came to making a decision about Jesus. He actually asked the question, "What am I to do with Jesus who is called Christ?" (Matthew 27:22 PHILLIPS).

Will you allow the fear of what *your* crowd will say to keep you from believing? Let me remind you of a more fearful prospect: that of eternity without God! Because I am deeply concerned about what you believe, and because I do want to be persuasive about these matters, I include the words of a preacher from another era. As he drew near to the conclusion of his sermon, he said:

> If the wondrous love of God in Jesus is not sufficient to attract you, then such is the value I attach to the worth of your soul that I will do my utmost to alarm you with the sight of the terrors of eternity without God—eternal remorse, eternal misery, eternal wretchedness—in a word, Hell.

So here is the most crucial question you will ever face: "Do you take this Savior?"

If your answer is "Yes," then let me encourage you to deal with the matter immediately. In Scotland, the congregation waits while the couple exit to sign their names to the marriage license. Away from all the clamor of the crowd, they seal their commitment to each other in a simple, private, indispensable moment. In years to come they will recall that day, and they may even uncover the document, but the strength of their marriage will be found not in a constant referral to the paperwork but in a steady commitment to the vows that they made. You may want to find a quiet place to seal your commitment. God is not so concerned with your ability to articulate your thoughts as He is aware of the sincerity of the response of your heart. A simple prayer such as that below may be of help to you in marking the moment. Depending on the kind of person you are, you may want to write this commitment in your journal or the flyleaf of your Bible. This is a unique occasion.

> Lord Jesus Christ, I confess that I am a guilty, lost, and helpless sinner. I want You to save me, to take Your rightful place as Lord of my life. I want to turn

from my sin and trust only in Your atoning sacrifice. I give my life to You. Take charge of it all and help me by the power of the Holy Spirit so to follow after You that I may one day hear You say, "Well done, good and faithful servant."

Since, as we have seen, faith is the gift of God, we may be absolutely confident that having given it, He will not take it back. Allow me to offer you the same encouragement Paul gave to the believers in Philippi: "[I am confident] of this, that he who began a good work in you will carry it on to completion until the day of Christ Jesus" (Philippians 1:6).

11

Solid Joys and Lasting Treasure

Praise be to the God and Father of our Lord Jesus Christ! In his great mercy he has given us new birth into a living hope through the resurrection of Jesus Christ from the dead, and into an inheritance that can never perish, spoil or fade—kept in heaven for you, who through faith are shielded by God's power until the coming of the salvation that is ready to be revealed in the last time" (1 Peter 1:3–5).

This is how Peter addresses the scattered Christians of his day. In the previous two verses he had recognized three facts that are true of every Christian. They are

1. chosen by God the Father,
2. cleansed by Christ's blood, and
3. sanctified by the Holy Spirit.

As he reflects upon this, it causes him to praise the Lord, and he explains to his readers that, although they may be suffering grief in facing trials, the basis of their rejoicing is to be found in pondering the wonder of their salvation. The prophets had been standing on their tiptoes wondering how the story would end, and the angels longed to look into these things.

Now this ties in with the story so far. Back in chapter 4 we saw how we can summarize the big picture in terms of the *good* as a description of the world as God created it; the *bad* as representing the world and our personal worlds as spoiled by sin; the *new* as expressing the transformation that takes place when we who were dead in transgressions were made alive in Christ; and the *perfect* as indicating what it will mean to be freed from sin's presence in the splendor of heaven. In a further attempt to summarize at least part of what's involved in being given "new birth into a living hope," we should think first in terms of . . .

CELEBRATION

"There is rejoicing in the presence of the angels of God over one sinner who repents" (Luke 15:10). Now this may simply be another way of referring to heaven, in which case the emphasis is this: God, who dwells in the presence of the angels, is a seeking God, who rejoices when even one sinner repents. Jesus made this very clear in telling His listeners three stories in succession about a lost sheep, a lost coin, and a lost boy. The context was one in which Luke tells us that the sinners were gathering around to hear Him, and the Pharisees were hanging around to criticize Him. Their complaint was: "This man welcomes sinners and eats with them" (v. 2). Ironically, in their expression of disgust they were telling the truth and putting the gospel in a nutshell.

In the first story, the shepherd searches for his

lost sheep, and when he returns carrying it on his shoulders, he calls his friends and neighbors to share his joy. In the second case, the rediscovery of a woman's lost coin becomes the occasion of rejoicing. In these two instances, Jesus explained that the earthly joy of rediscovery is pale in comparison to what takes place in heaven among the angels when even one sinner repents.

But it takes until the third story to provide a more adequate picture of the delight there is in heaven over the finding of the lost. Here the celebration is for the return of a son who by his departure had deprived his father of half his family. The music and dancing and the great meal and the new clothes all convey the sense of joy that had to be present on such an occasion. After all, the boy who'd been dead was alive; he had been lost and was found!

The extent to which the angels rejoice is not clear. We should not be surprised, however, that they do. After all, it was an angel who conveyed the good news when, on a routine evening in the pastures outside Bethlehem, the shepherds were terrified by his appearance and guided by his words. "Do not be afraid. I bring you good news of great joy that will be for all the people. Today in the town of David a Savior has been born to you; he is Christ the Lord" (Luke 2:10–11). When we add this to what we have already seen, we surely cannot rule out their rejoicing over a sinner's conversion.

While in the writings of other religions we discover man seeking ways to reach up to God, here in the uniqueness of the gospel we learn of One who comes seeking to save that which is lost. In direct contrast to the Pharisees, who were unwilling to rub shoulders with the publicans and sinners, Jesus cherished no fear of being polluted by them, and so He was ever willing to reach them. "The attitude of Jesus to publicans and sinners is not a mere humanitarian enthusiasm on His part: it is the manifestation of the will and purpose of God."[1]

There are few experiences in life that are capable of stirring such joyful emotions as the birth of a baby. Friends and neighbors gather and gaze, and the parents discover deep joy in the tiniest indications of the baby's progress. Those early days of celebration must inevitably give way to the more demanding challenges of teaching and training. There is more than a hint of sadness that comes with the awareness that the parental role is ultimately to prepare the youngster to be able to stand alone and eventually to be independent. While the early days have a lot of spoon feeding, the path to maturity demands participation on the child's part. Yet if the children are going to become useful members of society, they must learn to do things for themselves. There are certainly spiritual parallels when we think in terms of participation.

PARTICIPATION

"Like newborn babies, crave pure spiritual milk, so that by it you may grow up in your salvation" (1 Peter 2:2).

One of the clear evidences of a healthy infant is a good appetite. We should learn to be as regular in reading our Bibles as we are in eating our meals each day. The Bible is profitable for teaching us and correcting us and training us in the right way (2 Timothy 3:16). If we are to be adequately prepared to do the good works that God has planned for us (Ephesians 2:10), we must determine to be students of this book. It is important that we learn to *read* it and also that we *think* about it. In the first psalm we are introduced to one whose "delight is in the law of the Lord, and on his law he *meditates day and night* (Psalm 1:2, italics added).

In order to help us in this, God has given to His church pastor-teachers who have been given the unique gift and responsibility of expounding and applying God's Word to their people (1 Corinthians 12:28; Ephesians 4:7–13). Through preaching, God speaks to us, and because it is *His* Word brought into our minds and hearts by *His* Spirit (and not merely by the preacher), we discover that we learn to love the preaching that exalts God and humbles us as we live in submission to it. Such *hearing* of God's Word is to be accompanied by *doing*. James exhorts his readers: "Do not merely listen to the word, and so deceive yourselves. Do what it says" (James 1:22).

As we grow, we will become aware of the kinds of attitudes and habits which, if tolerated, will inhibit the rich growth God desires. Like soil that is too acidic is the life of the believer where anger, moral filth, evil, and pride are tolerated rather than obliterated.

"As you come to him, the living Stone—rejected by men but chosen by God and precious to him—you also, like living stones, are being built into a spiritual house to be a holy priesthood" (1 Peter 2:4–5).

Spiritual infants do not only require the right food, they need the security of a family. The Father's plan is that each of His children should be participating in the community of God's people. In other words, they should seek out a church fellowship where they can receive the kind of teaching and training that will lead them to maturity. While we come to Christ individually, we do not live in Him solitarily. In God's squadron it is all formation flying!

As a people belonging to God we declare His praises. The corporate worship of God's people is to be a fixed point in the Christian's life. We are not to view the times when God's family gets together as options but as joyful obligations. We should be able to say with the psalmist: "I was glad when they said to me, 'Let us go to the house of the Lord!'" (Psalm 122:1 NASB). Our participation should involve becoming members of a local church. In doing so, we are putting ourselves within the sphere of family discipline, we are asking to be shepherded, and we are able to discover and use the gifts God has given us for the benefit of the body. It is very important that we say no to isolation and yes to involvement.

It is within this context that we participate in the two sacraments Christ has given to the church: baptism and the Lord's Supper. In the first instance, having come to faith in Christ, we should declare this in baptism. Being baptized is in some ways like the wearing of a wedding ring insofar as it is a symbol of our having been united with Christ. It is a dramatic way of letting others know of the "change of ownership" that has, as we have said, taken place in our life. An unbaptized Christian is like a soldier without his uniform. We do not become Christians by being baptized. Our salvation is *pictured* in baptism; it is not *performed* by it.

By our participation in the Lord's Supper we are brought to a regular remembrance of the depth of God's love and mercy and we are encouraged to look forward to the day when we will share in the marriage supper of the Lamb. By these means we grow in the fear of the Lord which is the beginning of wisdom. Such loving and intimate reverence is a distinguishing feature of those who by God's grace are no longer slaves but sons and heirs (Galatians 4:6–7).

"Dear friends, I urge you, as aliens and strangers in the world, to abstain from sinful desires which war against your soul" (1 Peter 2:11). One of the things that often troubles the new believer is that while sin no longer reigns there is no question that it *remains*. While we have been saved from sin's *penalty*, and one day in heaven we will be saved from sin's *presence*, in the meantime we continue to stumble and fall. So we need to learn to run to God for forgiveness in much the same way children will run to the shelter and comfort of a father's forgiveness when they know themselves to have been in the wrong and are softened by the forgiveness of their father. At the same time, we need to become increasingly alert in identifying particular ways in which we find ourselves tempted. Every sin is an inside job. We cannot blame it on the big bad world or the devil's skill. We are each led away by our own individual desires. So we must recognize that repentance is not something that takes place only once at the outset of the Christian journey. It is, rather, a life of continuing repentance. The fact is, we need to be constantly turning from sin, and the more mature we become the more we know this to be the case. While Paul referred to himself early on as the "least of the apostles," by the close of his life he called himself "the chief of sinners"!

"Live such good lives among the pagans that . . . they may see your good deeds and glorify God" (1 Peter 2:12). As we participate in the family of God we are to bear witness to the dramatic difference Christ brings about in the lives of those who trust Him. Is it not striking that the environment in which Peter envisaged this taking place was "among the pagans." It seems clear that the apostle did not anticipate the Christians establishing the pattern of monasticism or the defensive strategy of the citadel. Rather, that in the rough and tumble of everyday life in society they would by their words and their deeds be ready to give an answer to everyone who asked them for an explanation of the hope they had (3:15). For while the pessimist may be looking down and the fearful, looking around, the Christian is to be one who lifts his eyes and looks up. For the Christian, the best is always still to come!

CONSUMMATION

One of the aspects of the Christian story that tends to receive less attention than it should is the Ascension of the Lord Jesus. Luke recorded how Jesus "was taken up before their very eyes, and a cloud hid him from their sight" (Acts 1:9). While the disciples were standing there, doubtless scratching their heads in wonder, two men dressed in white explained: "This same Jesus, who has been taken from you into heaven, will come back in the same way you have seen him go into heaven" (v. 11).

The writer of Hebrews encouraged the sometimes discouraged believers of his day by the reminder that, unlike the repetitious duties of the earthly priest, Jesus "had offered for all time one sacrifice for sins [and] sat down at the right hand of God" (Hebrews 10:12). While His death on the cross may have appeared to be a tragedy, it was the fulfillment of a divine strategy and established the fact of

Christ's victory over sin and death and hell. The diffi-
culties and tragedies and unanswered questions of
our lives must all be set against the backdrop of the
"big picture." The explanation the writer of Hebrews
gave for the incredible displays of faith recorded in
Hebrews 11 was this: "They admitted that they were
aliens and strangers on earth. . . . Instead, they were
longing for a better country—a heavenly one. Therefore God is not ashamed to be called their God, for
he has prepared a city for them" (Hebrews 11:13, 16).

It is this truth which underpins the hymn writer's
lyric:

> *Savior if of Zion's city,*
> *I through grace a member am,*
> *Let the world deride or pity,*
> *I will glory in Thy name.*
> *Fading is the worldling's pleasure,*
> *All his boasted pomp and show.*
> *Solid joys and lasting treasure*
> *None but Zion's children know.*

Earthly accolades, business success, whatever
may represent treasure to us, cannot bring satisfaction. Jesus warned His listeners not to lay up for
themselves treasures on earth because these will
eventually be eaten up or given up. They should
instead establish their investment portfolio in the
bank of heaven. There is nothing in the world that
is great enough to satisfy the longings of the human
heart. That is why the pursuit of pleasure for its
own sake is a dead-end street. The Scottish poet
Robert Burns captured the transience of it when he
wrote:

> But pleasures are like poppies spread—
> You seize the flow'r, its bloom is shed;
> Or like the snow falls in the river—
> A moment white—then melts for ever. . . .
> Or like the rainbow's lovely form,
> Evanishing amid the storm.
> *(Tam o'Shanter)*

THE PERFECT

Only lasting things can give us lasting pleasure. Only an eternal God can satisfy our need for eternal life. "For God so loved the world that he gave his one and only Son, that whoever believes in him shall not perish but have eternal life" (John 3:16). And the apostle John pulls back the curtain on the *perfect,* giving us a glimpse into the realm of solid joys and lasting treasure.

> I saw the Holy City, the new Jerusalem, coming down out of heaven from God, prepared as a bride beautifully dressed for her husband. And I heard a loud voice from the throne saying, "Now the dwelling of God is with men, and he will live with them. They will be his people, and God himself will be with them and be their God. He will wipe away every tear from their eyes. There will be no more death or mourning or crying or pain, for the old order of things has passed away."
>
> He who was seated on the throne said, "I am making everything new!" (Revelation 21:2–5)

For the Christian, the best is always yet to be. Earthly joys are touched with pain. Shadows are cast across our brightest days. Painful partings slowly prepare us for the ultimate parting that death will bring. Christian faith does not grant immunity from sadness and sickness, from bereavement and disappointment. At least not now! Those who suggest that it does mean the present enjoyment of health and wealth and peace and prosperity appeal to the general desire for well-being that marks our culture. But such a story is neither true to the Bible nor to human experience.

In an earlier generation, the church was accused of being so preoccupied with heaven that it had failed to take seriously the pressing matters of earth. In response to this charge that Christianity is just "pie in the sky when you die," Christians have pushed the pendulum to the opposite extreme. One doesn't hear much about heaven from the lips of messengers who are tailoring their message to appeal to a generation that expects to enjoy everything now. And, once again, the church misses the mark. Just when we have learned the importance of stressing the *now,* the culture is increasingly preoccupied with the *then.* Recent surveys reveal a fascination with heaven. In a recent poll 81 percent of those surveyed said they believed in the existence of heaven, where people live with God forever after they die. How you get there and what it will be like upon arrival remain a mystery for most.

It is here that the Bible helps us. There is a reserve in the descriptions it contains. John the apostle records his vision in broad brush strokes using dramatic imagery with special appeal to his first-century readers. The Christian's confidence about heaven is not granted by our ability to visualize it but is grounded in the total reliability of the One who promises it. "In my Father's house are many rooms; if it were not so, I would have told you" (John 14:2). Effective Christian living and sensible Christian preaching are tied in part to a right understanding of what the Bible says we can expect to experience *now* and what we look forward to enjoying *then*. In celebrating Communion, the Christian looks back to what has been accomplished by the death of Christ and looks forward to what will be enjoyed when we are reunited with Christ.

Sir Anthony Hopkins, the celebrated actor, speaks for more than himself when he says, "I love life because what more is there? Nothing lasts, really. There's going to be darkness, and it's all over." In direct contrast to this gloomy sentiment, the Christian discovers that death is not a cul-de-sac but a gateway into a brand new day. Isn't this an attractive proposition? An environment in which everything is new, not in the sense of modern, but that is pristine in its beauty, unfettered in its freedom, perfect in its purity. Our Creator has all the plans in place for a new heaven and a new earth that will be perfectly suited to our eternal existence.

When my children were younger, one of their most common bedtime questions was, "What will heaven be like?" Resisting the temptation to engage in speculation, I would tell them that it would be better than the best they could ever imagine. For their tiny minds that may have meant better than grandma's house or better than their birthday party or life without Monday mornings. I felt confident in making such a general statement, which seemed to be in keeping with the words of Paul in 1 Corinthians 2:9: "Eye hath not seen, nor ear heard, neither have entered into the heart of man, the things which God hath prepared for them that love him" (KJV).

The story is told of a street urchin who was taken from his urban setting to the country for the first time. Seeing a songbird on the branch of a tree, he commented, "Poor little bird, he has no cage to live in." His understanding (ours too) was governed by the life he knew, and that limited understanding caused him to make mistakes in his assessment of life outside his environment.

While there remains much that we cannot say, we have confidence in this. Eternal life with God in heaven will be . . .

A Life Without Loneliness

There will be no sense of being lost in the crowd. The ultimate companionship will be with God Himself. He who, having declared everything to be *good*, walked with Adam and Eve in the garden, will be our company when everything is *perfect*.

A Life Without Tears

What a prospect! The total extinction of heartache. No more tear-stained pillows of remorse. Kleenex obsolete! And this not as a result of our being able to pull ourselves together, but on account of the radical transformation that God Himself performs when the "perishable has been clothed with the imperishable, and the mortal with immortality" (1 Corinthians 15:54). The tears that have marked our sad good-byes will be more than compensated for by the welcome that awaits us and the reunions we will experience with unfading enjoyment.

A Life Without Death

Larry King lives comfortably by his skillful, winsome way of asking questions. But he admits to being most uncomfortable in the face of the one question for which he has not found a satisfying answer: What happens when you die? He fears death and is terrified of dying. He is clearly not unique in giving voice to this grave foreboding. As we have noted earlier, the gateway to eternal life is through the death of Jesus, who has taken in Himself death's sting for all who believe. In coming to Christ we receive the down payment of our eternal inheritance. The Holy Spirit guarantees all that is to come. In the past twenty-three years of pastoral ministry I have been humbled by the lives of those who have demonstrated this amazing confidence in the shadow of death. None more so than a young lady faced with the final stages of a degenerative disease who wrote the following letter:

Dear Mom, Dad, Family & Friends,

First and foremost, I want to tell you how much I love you and how grateful I am for the love and care you have given me. It isn't easy thinking about leaving you, but since we know that time is approaching, I would like to share some requests with you and trust you will carry them out.

My hope is that this will make a difficult time a little easier for everyone and it will help you, knowing what pleasure it gives me. . . . I have requested that my pastor, Alistair Begg, conduct a simple memorial service. I would like a closed casket, perhaps with some pictures.

It is difficult expressing all that this life and my future eternal life mean to me. This verse expresses a little of my feelings and my gratitude to God for the life, the family and the friends He has given me.

"You gave me life and showed kindness,
 and in Your providence watched over my spirit."
(Job 10:12)

It is strange yet appropriate that I am writing this to you on Independence Day, for I am anticipating the day when I will be truly free in the Lord.

Please celebrate my homecoming with me.

If I were Larry King, I would want to find out what made it possible for Diane to write as she did. I should want to know whoever she knew, if in the knowing of them such confidence was produced in the face of our final enemy.

A Life Without Pain

Instead of suggesting, as some do, that pain is an illusion, the Bible acknowledges that it is a reality. While some seek to banish it in the name of the Lord, the Bible actually affirms its place in the purposes of God. As philosophers struggle with the question, Why do bad things happen to good people? the Bible turns that question on its head. Here is another instance in which an awareness and acceptance of the "big picture" is the path to peace. The biblical record and human history combine to make perfectly clear that there is much that is inexplicable about the often fierce intensity of mental, physical, and emotional pain on the journey of life. Rather than attempting to dance around the question, the Bible tells us that the answer lies not in the *now* but in the *then*. This is hard for a generation that has grown up believing that instant gratification is our right and always best to accept. But in recognizing that the answer does not lie in the adult nature of our doubts, but in the childlike nature of our trust, we will be saved from anger, bitterness, or silly notions. One day in heaven we will be free from all pain, including the painful task of trying to unravel the mystery.

A World Without End

The old order of things is finite. Heaven takes us into the realm of the infinite. Now I write these words with the pressure of a deadline. There will be no such phraseology in heaven. It will be meaningless. We should not think of this in terms of a long, lazy Sunday afternoon. It is too wonderful for human language to adequately describe. Hymn writers have done their best but have flirted with sentimentality or have failed to focus our attention on God and His glory by filling our thoughts with the benefits that await us.

There are many wonderful moments in a wedding ceremony. None more dramatic than the moment when the groom looks down the aisle seeing his bride as she begins to process to his side. In talking with the men about those moments, it is no surprise to me that they find it almost impossible to describe what their bride was wearing or even actually how she wore her hair. They were so taken up with the fact of *her* that they lost sight of virtually everything else besides. They certainly were oblivious to the flower arrangements!

It is this thought which runs through the hymn that Annie Cousins wrote as a result of reading the memoirs of the godly Samuel Rutherford.

> The bride eyes not her garment,
>   But her dear bridegroom's face;
> I will not gaze at glory,
>   But on my King of grace;

Not at the crown He giveth,
But on His piercèd hand:
The Lamb is all the glory
Of Immanuel's land.

The allegory of John Bunyan has arguably never been bettered. Few books written in 1678 are still in print three hundred and twenty years later. The final picture he paints of the sojourners Christian and Hopeful is so attractive that he tells us that he wished he could join them.

Now I saw in my dream, that these two men went in at the gate; and lo! as they entered, they were transfigured; and they had raiment put on, that shone like gold. . . .

. . . I looked in after them, and behold, the City shone like the sun; the streets also were paved with gold: and in them walked many with crowns on their heads, palms in their hands, and golden harps. . . .

There were also of them that had wings, and they answered one another without intermission, saying, "Holy, holy, holy is the Lord!" And after that, they shut up the gates, which then I had seen, I wished myself among them.

And what then of you, the reader? Do you wish yourself among them? Inclusion in that company is not something we struggle to earn. The gift of God is eternal life in Jesus Christ our Lord. Have you ever accepted the gift?

Notes

Chapter 1: Mocha, Biscotti, and the Search for Meaning

1. Neale Walsch, *Conversations with God* (New York: Putnam, 1996).

2. "Dr. Gallup's Finger on America's Pulse," *Economist*, 27 September 1997.

3. Russell Chandler, *Understanding the New Age* (Dallas: Word, 1988), 20.

4. Harold A. Netland, *Dissonant Voices* (Grand Rapids: Eerdmans, 1991), 7, citing Chandler.

5. Ralph Lapp, cited in Os Guinness, *Dust of Death* (London: Inter-Varsity, 1973), 67.

6. Guinness, *Dust of Death*, 16.

7. Quoted in Guinness, *Dust of Death*, 36.

8. Michael Green, *Critical Choices* (Leicester, England: Inter-Varsity, 1995), 55.

9. Nancy Gibbs, "Angels Among Us," *Time*, 27 December 1993.

10. Deirdrie Donahue, "A Haven for the Intellect," *USA Today*, 10 July 1997.

11. Howard Schultz, *Pour Your Heart into It* (New York: Hyperion, 1997), 12.

Chapter 2: Meanwhile, Back in Athens

1. I. Howard Marshall, *The Acts of the Apostles* (Leicester, England: Inter-Varsity, 1980), 281.
2. Suze Orman, *The 9 Steps to Financial Freedom* (New York: Crown, 1997).
3. Michael Green, *Critical Choices* (Leicester, England: Inter-Varsity, 1995), 18.
4. Kenneth F. W. Prior, *The Gospel in a Pagan Society* (Downers Grove, Ill.: InterVarsity, 1975), 44.
5. Sinclair B. Ferguson, *The Pundit's Folly* (Carlisle, Pa.: Banner of Truth, 1995), 38.
6. F. F. Bruce, *The Book of Acts* (London: Marshall Morgan and Scott, 1962), 351.
7. Alister McGrath, *Bridge-Building* (Leicester, England: Inter-Varsity, 1992), 53.
8. C. S. Lewis, *Screwtape Proposes a Toast* (London: Collins, 1965), 97–98.

Chapter 3: Glorious Ruins

1. J. I. Packer, *Concise Theology* (Wheaton, Ill.: Tyndale, 1993), 81.
2. Alister McGrath, *Bridge-Building* (Leicester, England: Inter-Varsity, 1992), 181.
3. Derek J. Prime, *This Way to Life*, 32.
4. J. I. Packer, *Knowing God* (Downers Grove, Ill.: InterVarsity, 1973), 171.
5. Bruce Milne, *Know the Truth* (Downers Grove, Ill.: InterVarsity, 1982), 106.
6. Cf. McGrath, *Bridge-Building*, 181.
7. T. H. Huxley, quoted in Michael Green, *Running from Reality* (Downers Grove, Ill.: InterVarsity, 1983), 88.
8. Packer, *Concise Theology*, 82.
9. Michael Horton, *The Law of Perfect Freedom* (Chicago: Moody, 1993), 42.
10. James Patterson and Peter Kim, *The Day America Told the Truth* (New York: Plume, 1992).
11. Milne, *Know the Truth*, 114.

Chapter 4: The Big Picture

1. Michael Green, *Critical Choices* (Leicester, England: Inter-Varsity, 1995), 46.

2. John Polkinghorne, *The Way the World Is* (London: SPCK, 1983), 12.

3. Alister McGrath, *Bridge-Building* (Leicester, England: Inter-Varsity, 1992), 62; on the Five Ways, cf. Colin Brown, *Philosophy and the Christian Faith* (Leicester, England: Inter-Varsity, 1986), 20–32; and Keith E. Yandell, *Christianity and Philosophy* (Grand Rapids: Ecrdmans, 1984), 48–97.

4. Polkinghorne, *The Way the World Is,* 33.

5. Bruce Milne, *Know the Truth* (Downers Grove, Ill.: InterVarsity, 1982), 133.

6. Green, *Critical Choices,* 70.

7. John R. W. Stott, *Basic Christianity* (Downers Grove, Ill.: Inter-Varsity, 1971), 50.

8. McGrath, *Bridge-Building,* 31.

9. Milne, *Know the Truth,* 133.

10. McGrath, *Bridge-Building,* 163.

Chapter 5: More Than a Man

1. Alister McGrath, *Bridge-Building* (Leicester, England: Inter-Varsity, 1992), 176.

2. Derek J. Prime, *Jesus, His Life and Ministry* (Nashville: Thomas Nelson, 1995), 11.

3. J. I. Packer, *I Want to Be a Christian* (Eastbourne, U.K.: Kingsway, 1977), 39.

4. C. S. Lewis, preface to *The Screwtape Letters,* with *Screwtape Proposes a Toast,* rev. ed. (New York: Macmillan, 1961), x.

Chapter 6: A Matter of Life and Death

1. C. S. Lewis, *Mere Christianity* (New York: Macmillan, 1952), 41.

2. Quoted in Michael Green, *Critical Choices* (Leicester, England: Inter-Varsity, 1995), 31.

3. John R. W. Stott, *Basic Christianity* (Downers Grove, Ill.: Inter-Varsity, 1971), 27.

4. Derek J. Prime, *This Way to Life,* 43.

5. Stott, *Basic Christianity,* 36.

6. Kirstie Alley, Interview, *USA Today*, 11 December 1997, Life section, 9D.

7. J. I. Packer, *Knowing God* (Downers Grove, Ill.: InterVarsity, 1973), 51.

8. H. E. Guillebaud, *Why the Cross?* (Chicago: InterVarsity, 1947), 130, 185.

9. R. B. Kuiper, *God-Centered Evangelism* (Carlisle, Pa.: Banner of Truth, 1994), 155.

10. Prime, *This Way to Life*, 48.

11. Ibid.

12. Alec Motyer, *Look to the Rock* (Leicester, England: Inter-Varsity, 1996), 85.

13. Ibid.

14. Charles Haddon Spurgeon, *Advice for Seekers* (reprint; Carlisle, Pa.: Banner of Truth, 1993), 51.

Chapter 7: The Ultimate Scandal

1. Nathaniel Micklem, in John R. W. Stott *Christ the Controversialist* (Downers Grove, Ill.: InterVarsity, 1970, 1978), 129.

2. Charles Haddon Spurgeon, *Advice for Seekers* (reprint; Carlisle, Pa.: Banner of Truth, 1993), 58.

3. T. W. Manson, in Norval Geldenhuys, *Commentary on the Gospel of Luke* (Grand Rapids: Eerdmans, 1951), 403.

4. John Bunyan, *The Pilgrim's Progress* (reprint; Westwood, N.J.: Barbour), 44.

Chapter 8: Settling the Accounts

1. Bruce Hilton, "Death Now Society's Only Taboo Topic," Cleveland *Plain Dealer*, 29 June 1996, 6E

2. Peter Cotterell, *This Is Christianity* (Leicester, England: Inter-Varsity, 1985), 103.

3. James Montgomery Boice, *Foundations of the Faith* (Downers Grove, Ill.: InterVarsity, 1986), 712.

4. Cotterell, *This Is Christianity*, 107.

Chapter 9: Forgiveness—Friendship—Focus

1. J. I. Packer, *Knowing God* (Downers Grove, Ill.: InterVarsity, 1973), 170.

2. Eugene Kennedy, Interview, "Why a Good Friend Is Hard to Find," *U.S. News & World Report*, 1983.

3. Derek J. Prime, *This Way to Life*, 63.

4. Harvey Penick and Bud Shrake, *Harvey Penick's Little Red Book* (New York: Simon & Schuster, 1992), 45.

Chapter 10: Coming to Christ

1. Alister McGrath, *Bridge-Building* (Leicester, England: Inter-Varsity, 1992), 79.

2. Leon Morris, *The Gospel According to John* (Grand Rapids: Eerdmans, 1971, 1981), 99.

3. John Murray, *The Collected Writings of John Murray*, vol. 2, *Select Lectures in Systematic Theology* (Carlisle, Pa.: Banner of Truth, 1977, 1984), 237.

4. Sinclair B. Ferguson, *The Christian Life* (London: Hodder & Stoughton, 1981), 61.

5. John R. W. Stott, *God's New Society* (Leicester, England: Inter-Varsity, 1979), 83.

6. Ferguson, *The Christian Life*.

7. Ibid., 67.

8. Dietrich Bonhoeffer, *The Cost of Discipleship* (New York: Macmillan, 1963), 79.

Chapter 11: Solid Joys and Lasting Treasure

1. T. W. Manson in Norval Geldenhuys, *Commentary on the Gospel of Luke* (Grand Rapids: Eerdmans, 1951), 403.